TO
Ky

WHEN YOU STAND UP TO THE SUN

Deanna

and at the end of the day,
Nothing will delight her soul
More than dancing wildly
in the free blowing Wind.

Enjoy the adventure! Pages
to come...

WHEN
YOU STAND UP
TO THE SUN

DEANNA AMODEO

NEW DEGREE PRESS

COPYRIGHT © 2020 DEANNA AMODEO

WHEN YOU STAND UP TO THE SUN

ISBN   978-1-63676-537-2 *Paperback*
          978-1-63676-087-2 *Kindle Ebook*
          978-1-63676-088-9 *Ebook*

Dedication

This book is dedicated to my mother and father, Moo and Charles. They knew they were to have a daughter but didn't know of the boldness she would harbor. Thank you Mom and Dad for this sweet life you have given me.

This book is also dedicated to New Degrees Press, for having the patience and tolerance to deal with the turbulent lifestyle that has led to the creation of my first novel.

TABLE OF CONTENTS

———

INTRODUCTION

THE SMILING FOOL

For what reason are we put on this earth?

That's a bold one to ask, isn't it?

Perhaps you can sum this inquiry up in a brief sentence or two.

Or perhaps not.

For eons, human beings have spent a great deal of time grabbing foolishly at concepts that float just above their heads, convincing themselves that they most certainly have found the one solid answer to life on earth.

Fools.

But I confess: I am also a fool at such endeavors.

I've climbed mountains, voyaged dutifully across continents, and rested my weary head under the fading stars, only to pursue the alluring fantasy of this question: for what reason do I exist?

After enough time exhausting myself with the perplexities of life, watching how people rise and fall, suffer and conquer, I decided chasing such a question would cost me the very answer that I seek. So I've fallen, on my hands and knees, in surrender to the two answers which best fit a heart-wrenched gypsy like me:

1. Interacting with other humans
2. Gaining life experience in honor of creating stories

This leads us to the question: is everyone's purpose here on earth the same?

That's where things get tricky. That's where my wisdom falls flat on its face.

I don't have that answer for you.

But what I do have is the humble telling of my story that reaches straight through the belly of my vulnerability to grab at the heart of my experiences.

I invite you, human to human, on this Fool's journey to share where I've fallen, to share where I've risen, in hopes of inspiring you to take in the culmination of both your mistakes and your might so that you can surrender to your purpose here on Earth.

I'll be honest in saying, it ain't always pretty.

It ain't always perfect.

But it's human, and it's real.

Before we can commence this journey, I humbly invite you to meet a few of the requirements I was asked to meet when I set off on these travels.

The first is that you turn around now and check the weight of the baggage you are harboring behind you. To transverse across this journey together, you'll need space in your "soul-pack." So please, here and now, take only what you need, empty out the aged burdens holding you down and the preconceptions holding you back. Give yourself ample space to be open enough to receive the contents of this book.

The second thing I ask of you is that you call yourself a Fool and be willing to smile while doing so.

The Fool always smiles because the Fool always knows, that life is but an adventure.

Now that we stand on the same ground, allow me to introduce myself. My name is Deanna, born a Jersey girl at best. I was raised under the strict scrutiny of a Sicilian American family, spending my spare time throughout adolescence watching my brothers wrestle, eating copious amounts of pasta, and imitating my father's Brooklyn accent. Nothing special here. After so many years of this nonsense, I had no choice but to flee the dread of a planned life, in hopes of carelessly vagabonding the world, all the while earning the title of the Fool.

Yes, I admit it.

I am a Fool.

But not the kind of Fool who spends Saturday evenings at the bar betting on pre-recorded dog races. Or the kind of Fool who puts an ice cream cake in the pantry.

I am referring to the Fool as the tarot does—the one who is both the adventurer and the adventure itself.

The tarot deck contains twenty-one cards in the major arcana. All the cards in this arcana represent significant life lessons with their influences on the karmic play of life. In this arcana you can pull cards like the High Priestess, the Lovers, or Death. Each card is numbered in accordance to when it appears on the soul's journey of evolution. There is one card, however, that is unnumbered, thus signifying it commences the journey, ends the journey, and embodies the journey throughout all of its entirety. It is the main character in the major arcana.

That card is the Fool.

Numbered zero for unlimited potential. Numbered zero to be presented in every moment.

As depicted on the tarot card imagery, the Fool is standing on a cliff edge whimsically stepping forward as if to take a grand leap of faith. The gaze of the Fool is lifted toward the light of day, and she carries everything she needs over her shoulders. You could call her a minimalist.

The Fool is unaware of what unknown territories lie ahead, but she is aware of the voyage she is about to take, and greets it with delight and wonder. In her hand she holds a rose, which symbolizes an intentional innocence and purity of being. The mountains beyond her represent the lessons and challenges yet to come, which does not put her in a state of unease but rather a state of curiosity in beginning her long-awaited exploration.

There you have it.

This wonderful description embodies the past years of my voyages across the world.

I pride myself in being this Fool; you know why?

Because the Fool is the one who encounters the journey, takes on the adventures, and thus creates the stories. The Fool willingly trusts life with an innocence that is not naive, but intentional, because learning is desired.

***

In my early twenties, I took the Fool's journey by leaving the sweet suburbs of my childhood home in honor of an expedition. I left perfection, planning, and programming out of my suitcase, as I asked you to do as well, and I curiously put one foot in front of the other, greeting anything that crossed my path with grace and a smile.

What did I come across?

Humans.

I came across humans.

Can you believe it? Humans on planet earth!

A whole boatload of them.

Yapping. Eating. Grumbling. Laughing.

Singing. Dancing, Playing. Sharing.

Crying. Cooking. Crafting.

Humans.

And these humans also came across me, the smiling Fool.

Some humans I adored for their vigorous spirits and hearty souls.

Some humans bored me with their lack of amusement.

Some humans taught me how to be a better human by embodying qualities that have transformed the world-wide community.

Some humans taught me how not to be by treating others with disrespect and judgment.

Some humans, like you, gave me their undivided attention as I spoke with them, cried to them, and joked with them, while some humans received my undivided attention as they took my hand, cooked for me, and looked into my eyes.

I love it all—the humanness and the rawness of emotion.

The foolishness of life on earth.

But throughout my Fool's journey, I came to adore one thing more than anything else in this world. I've become enamored with the stories that pour, cascade, and erupt out of these magnificent human beings, and the stories I created alongside them.

Stories are our scent. They leave behind a trail by which we can be followed, sought after, and discovered. They are what make us unique from our neighbors, siblings, and parents. And not to mention they are timeless, in the sense that tribes, cultures, and people across the globe have been coming together to share stories since human-hood was ever a thing.

Why stories?

Because they simply are what make us human.

And humans make stories.

You see that?

Stories and humans go together like skin and flesh. Humans are the skin that presents itself to the world and stories are the flesh that fill the spaces beneath our meek surfaces.

So, as I take you on this Fool's journey across the mountains and through the waters, I will share with you not only the flesh of my story, but the body of others' stories as well.

In the pages to come, you will encounter a story which has been co-created, weaved, and embedded within the stories of four other humans.

Only four humans?

Well, goddamn.

I can't write about everyone I met and interacted with!

So, I chose the four most altering human relationships I've encountered throughout these travels, the romantic stories with the most flesh, the four other Fools with the biggest smiles who happened to teach me how to embody wholeness while living in this world.

Despite the various countries they come from, the different languages they speak, and the diverse social economic backgrounds they were raised in, these four humans actually have one wildly significant thing in common.

C'mon, the answer is simple here:

The Fool.

Or should I say beautiful, foolish me?

These four men have nothing in common except for the mere fact they once adored me, the Fool.

I also adored them because they put me through heaven and hell and gave me the vision to write this story.

So, now that you know me *oh so well*, let me introduce you to those four other humans whose presence and adventurous souls helped to shape the Fool that I am today.

***

Meet Air, born near the end of September, when the Libra season is just breezing through, to a Mormon mother and an atheist father. Air was raised with little discipline, so he took to the streets at a young age with his neighborhood friends and their rusted skateboards. Through the large cityscape of Salt Lake City they would cruise from dusk till dawn, avoiding religion while following trends. He spent his time drifting without an agenda, ready to encounter the alluring and dainty qualities of life, until his freedom was taken from him when his health faltered, big time, with no known causes.

Meet Water, brought into this world on a cold February day in Paris during the time of the emotional and intuitive Pisces season. Water was a rebel since day one, always challenging his family, the way things are done on Earth, and the reasoning behind them. Water became a man of spontaneous expression by committing to "go with the flow" on the other side of the world after his aunt purchased him a one-way ticket to Buenos Aires for his seventeenth birthday.

Meet Earth, a springtime child born in a land of eternal spring itself. He came bold and ready right smack in the middle of May, as grounded and stubborn as any Taurus baby could ever be. His early childhood was a blur, and he still has never seen a photo of his childhood self, nor does he know the exact year he was born. Earth became street smart, but frequently proved to be a living model of a "smart kid doing stupid things." All the while, he kept himself alive long enough to travel out of and away from the ghetto life of Guatemala City.

Meet Fire, born directly on the hour when Cancer season hands over the torch to Leo season. Son to a migrant Mexican family, he grew up in the sweet Georgia suburbs, living a childhood completely opposite to the ones his parents had endured. Education and concentration did not come easy, so Fire was delighted when he graduated high school with a steady 2.0 GPA and was handed the keys to his father's well-developed business. Fire grew burnt out, sick, and overworked by the time he reached his early twenties, which left him to make one big decision: abandon all he has ever known.

***

Yes, they all have names. But isn't referring to them as the elements that correlate to their astrological sign so much more fun? Not to mention the levels of lessons I learned through my interactions with them are congruent to the qualities of the elements themselves. There were challenging moments for sure, and times I had wanted to give up, rid myself of amusement and "go home." But I stayed humble, open, and foolish, willing to learn my lessons and carry onward.

I never said the Fool's journey would be an easy one, and as a matter of fact, the more open I was on my travels, the more people, situations, and challenges came to greet and test me. Through this, I've noted how we frequently have set ideas of how we want our journeys to be, but life always has different plans because how can we possibly know what we don't know and are in need of learning? I no longer believe our lives are predestined, but they are interactive with the level of energy, openness, and willingness we offer outwardly.

As you find yourself reading my humble journey of Fool-Hood, I ask that you keep a keen eye on the way I tell my story, observing the purposeful naive actions I took in a shameless state, and the creative ways I learned from them.

I attempted to maintain an "upright" Fool as much as possible, venturing through the unknown. I share with you the bare bones and all so that you can potentially feel a rise of liberation to turn around and greet your life with a new set of Foolish eyes, all without judgment.

An Upright Fool:

- Greets the known and unknown world with a smile and a willingness to learn.
- Encourages traveling through the unknown self.
- Learns a lesson from everyone they encounter.
- Allows situations, relationships, and voyages to turn out as they may.

A Reversed Fool:

- Lets lack of experience or trust alter decisions.
- Worries, plans, or longs for perfection.
- Judges others and fears the loss of control.
- Gets angry and frustrated when outcomes reveal themselves.

If you find yourself in the realm of a "Reversed Fool," constantly worrying, trying to control, and running from your dreams or aspirations, don't be alarmed; you are not alone. I was once a reversed Fool and I will tell you that you can *always* find a way to bring the Fool upright. I did, and so can you.

What you must do is:

1. Drop everything you thought you've ever known.
2. Let go of the idea of how life should be.
3. Be curious.
4. Just take one step into the abyss—the unknown territory, the shadow—with me, here and now.

SHADOW DANCING

Here I am.

Beautiful, joyous me!

How lucky I am to be alive, to harness this supple female body, this creative mind, this positive outlook on life.

Here I am, and I'm going to live my life the way I want!

I won't listen to my parents.

I refuse to burden myself with society.

And I certainly don't plan on attending college in this lifetime.

I want something different—an adventure, to be an example.

For people to look up at me and say, "Deanna, what even *is* your life?"

I'm ready.

I walk through the university's heavy doors with a stack of books and slam them down on the desk in front of my radiology professor.

"I'm done. I'm leaving the program."

"But Deanna, you've been doing so goo—"

The door closes.

I walk into the primary-colored ice cream shop with a paper bag of black cotton tees in my grip, and I place it down on the counter.

"I'm done. I'm leaving this job."

"But Deanna...you are on schedule for tonigh—"

The door closes.

I go to my childhood home and I sell my belongings—the beautiful, tight black dresses, the knitted scarves, and the dainty decor.

I will keep *only* what I need from here on out.

I pack my backpack and walk downstairs to dismiss my parents.

"I'm done. I'm leaving this town."

"But Deanna...what about your famil—"

The door closes.

***

Now, you see I am happy!

Happy as a clam, for I have the whole wide world to myself and my own essence is a pearl, a charm.

No longer will I need to study a boring subject.

No longer will I work like a slave, ice cream dripping down my white pants for minimum wage.

No longer will I do what my parents tell me to do.

I'm free and I'm standing up for my *own* self.

My own sunshine.

My own light.

"What a good life this will be, now that I don't have any distractions."

I know my spirit has my back, as she shines her ethereal rays onto my body.

Her light surrounds me, glimmering and glistening, like an angel's first breath.

The strength of her blaze penetrates my mortal human flesh.

"What a good life this will be, now that it's just me."

My spirit hovers directly above the crown of my head, cascading her precious light in my direction.

I feel free.

I am free.

In this freedom, I'm safe to be who I'm meant to be, and so I decide to let loose and dance.

I decide to dismiss it all.

I praise myself for having done what I've done.

For leaving my *old* life behind.

"What a good life this will be, now that everything is better."

This is the life I've *always* wanted.

One without boundaries.

I let loose and roar with joy, play like a wild woman on ecstasy.

My heart flares open, absorbing the fullness of just simply being alive.

Of simply being human!

I'm no longer aware of time because I'm liberated!

I'm free to dance and frolic underneath the heavenly rays.

I'm unaware of how long I spend in this state of ecstasy.

It could have been seconds, or lifetimes.

But it doesn't matter!

Because I'm free.

I'm *so free*, I dare not notice what's going on around me.

I'm *so free*, that I am oblivious.

Until I hear a loud and grumbling ripple from behind me, a roar of thunder.

My attention is grabbed.

My dancing stops.

I turn slowly, a big smile upon my face, stunned from all that dancing in that light.

My eyes adjust to the scene before me. I notice the ominous shape of a dark cloud coming out from over the horizon. The figure makes its way through the sky, towering overhead like a grand skyscraper, attempting, I believe, to intimidate me and halt my joyful flow.

But I'm so free this darkness doesn't frighten me. Rather, it intrigues.

The dark abyss stands before me, hovering and floating like an entitled boss.

"What are you?" I ask.

"What are you?" it replies.

"Can't you tell what I am?" I hiss.

"Yes. You're a Fool."

The dark cloud roars with laughter, killing my vibe.

"What did you say?"

"I said *YOOUUU* are a *FOOOL*," it teases.

"And why is that?" I ask in defense.

"Because you are open to an adventure, aren't you?"

It awaits my response, which I don't have.

"Don't tell me that you don't know of Fools and adventurers? They are of the same accord, darling."

Now I'm confused.

"Tell me, do you not know who—or shall I say what—I am?"

I take a moment to see the sight before my eyes for what it is, as the sun still glares directly over my head. I squint my eyes and take a step closer, then another, and another.

Each time I step forward, the ominous figure steps backward.

Until I realize.

I realize exactly what it is.

"Are you my shadow?"

"Cast from your very own light, my dear."

"Oh. Shit."

"You're not kidding. You're shadow dancing now, beauty."

I stand frozen with anticipation as the boisterous shadow begins to twist and turn before me, wildly altering shapes and sizes.

It's quite the large thing, this shadow.

Did I really cast that?

Have I been so ignorant as not to notice?

Maybe I am a *Fool*.

With one great force, one mighty implosion, the shadow before me spontaneously bursts open. Its rupture shakes the ground and sends me backward a few steps. Baffled and all the more perplexed, I watch as four sublime figures emerge from its core.

"What the fuc—"

My jaw drops as the four figures materialize out before me, taking on the outlined shapes of human forms. One of the figures whips around, so whimsical in nature it nearly makes me dizzy. I glance toward another whose presence is fluid and pulsing like a throbbing ocean. My sight is caught by the rooted boldness of the third figure. Lastly, I turn my gaze to the fourth figure, whose embodiment burns brightly.

The scene takes me a moment to process, as it's not every day that a giant black cloud, my shadow, comes to greet me, tossing figurines all over the place. The only way I can describe what I'm looking at, is that these four ominous shapes seem to embody the elements: air, water, earth, and fire.

The figures step forward one at a time, beginning to present their diverse qualities to me as they materialize into the bodies of four young men. My heart becomes frantic. I most definitely feel a strange and subtle draw to each of them in different ways. My cheeks flush hot. My stomach flutters. They are beautiful, perfect, even—just my type.

"Have I gone mad?" I run my hands over my face and through my hair.

"No, you haven't," the sweet voice of my spirit answers from above.

"You have chosen this path. Go on. They will teach you something."

"But *who* are they?"

"Well, you tell me."

With that, the voice of my spirit fades and the light of her sun dims ever so slightly, allowing me a clearer vision of what stands before me.

***

I look at the men standing within the shadow, each one personifying his own element.

They *are beautiful* indeed.

My heart flutters at the long and lean frame of Air. His hair in dark, thick curls, face sculpted ever so. His eyes are warm and inviting, his stature whimsical and dainty. He wears a decorated vest showing his bare chest.

I'm intrigued by Water. I can tell that he is ready. For what? I don't know. But whatever it is, he's ready for it. He's on a mission, that I can surely tell. With a decorated band wrapped around his head, his hair is pushed away from his face. He wears no shoes.

I look lovingly toward Earth. He's smiling the biggest smile I've ever seen a man wear. His hair is knotted, styled, and playfully kept in a beanie. His skin is dark and supple, and his stance is secure.

Finally, I observe Fire. He stands in a perfected posture, wearing a layer of thin black clothing, resting his hands behind his back. His shoulders are relaxed, and his face is calm.

"So, tell me, are you ready?" the shadow speaks.

"Ready for what? Is this a sick joke?"

"This isn't a joke, Deanna. You're a Fool, and so you must learn, voyage, and grow like one. You have danced in the light of your spirit for far too long, being ignorant to what stands behind you. I'm your shadow, and these four men come through me to teach you a lesson that your precious little light *cannot* and *will not* teach you. If you really want to *play*, if you really want to be *free*, then summon the courage and step on forward."

"No! I refuse. This is asinine!"

As the words leave my clenched jaw, a strong gust of wind begins to blow, picking up rapid speed. No longer do I have the strength to stand my ground. I'm too easily swayed by the wind. I'm being blown away. I try to resist. I try to fight the strong pull, but I cannot.

I'm tossed, thrown, and throttled forward.

I land directly into the embracing arms of Air, already mesmerized and distracted by his ample beauty.

"You're beautiful..."

AIR

THE LONE WOLF

—

The full-ish Moon hovers herself in the darkened sky above Salt Lake City. It's springtime in Utah, where the wildflowers grace one's ankle, the birds call with heavenly delight, and the temperature begins increasing to a boil. As the Moon takes a moment to cherish her mighty view, she sings and hums her usual Moon songs, conjuring a melody of simple joy. The night-time sky hums with her sound, a sound many humans don't notice. All the way down on planet Earth, a moving streak happens to catch the Moon's eye, distracting her from chanting. Moon wavers her attention by engaging with this interesting sight.

"Oh. What is this I see?"

She squints her eyes and zooms in, using her height as a vantage point to further observe the scene taking place just two hundred forty thousand miles below.

The aged gaze of the Moon falls upon a rather curious and youthful young man, one she is not unfamiliar with. She's been keeping a keen eye on this man throughout most of his upbringing because he's always been a creature of the night. During his most fundamental years of growth, he spent much time in solitude reading stories of ancient Samurais, Native

Americans, and lost leaders, all while resting underneath the luminous moonlight. The Moon adores him, as you would imagine a wise grandmother would, for the qualities of his supple mind and quivering heart.

She's given him a nickname that makes her laugh so.

The nickname "*The Lone Wolf.*"

The Moon, now in a state of full ecstasy, longs to see this precious human even closer, so what does she do? She squints and narrows her captivated eyes, acquiring a better view. There he is, the Lone Wolf, with his right foot placed atop an exquisite floating board and his left foot swinging back and forth.

"He always does this," Moon thinks to herself. "He always glides across the cityscape like a shooting star."

The Moon is both distracted from her lunar duties and enamored by her earthly vantage point.

"Oh! If I am to be the queen of my own phases, I may just need to have an even closer look!" Her enchanted voice whistles to nothing and no one in particular, as she permits herself the ability to zoom in more, able now to see the details of his young and determined face.

Her hypnotic glare extends through to the solemn streets of Salt Lake City, stirring up curiosity in the sky, and she is shaken when a deep voice calls from far out in the distance.

"Dearest Moon. Please, tell me. What do you see?" the constellation Libra asks from one hundred and eighty-five light-years away.

"Oh, Libra! If it isn't you. It's been so long, way too many light-years, since I've heard your proper voice. I will tell you, Libra. I just happened to know, deep within my soul, you would be intrigued by this rather *curious* young man," Moon boasts of her intuitive side.

The Moon settles her attention back on the quick-moving scene from before, relaying now what she is witnessing.

"Oh, Libra. I see the Lone Wolf having a rather extraordinary evening by himself. Once again, though it seems!" she hoots and hollers, a cackle in her voice.

"What makes this evening extraordinary?" Libra bellows from afar.

"Oh, dear Libra. That's a rather insightful question, but I'll have to concentrate even more. Give me a moment, if I may." Moons words are lengthy and drawn out like the exaggerated voice of a ridiculous crone.

"Oh, well. Now I see! What makes this evening so extraordinary, Libra, is that the Lone Wolf is determined to arrive somewhere. I see more clearly now the magical device on which he moves."

"Well, where exactly is he going?" Libra demands to know.

"Libra, you do ask all the right questions now." Moon chuckles and concentrates the hardest she has ever had to in the eternity of her being, squinting as much as she possibly can for her ripe old age.

"You won't believe this. He's just arrived at his destination. By gosh, Libra, it's an open field! In the field I see hundreds and hundreds of flowers. Now, they must be wildflowers, for no human would have such energy to have planted all of these!" Moon chants on and on. "Libra, you are so far away, and you may not believe my words, but the Lone Wolf is on his hands and knees. Whatever is he doing?" Moon sighs deeply, ignorant to what she is watching.

"Tell me, Moon, quickly, who does he pray to?" The constellation Libra, from so far away, already knows and begins to grow anxious with curiosity because the Lone Wolf is a child of his, and Libra suspects that this young man is in need of guidance.

Just as Libra's question reaches the Moon's light year, she nearly rolls over in her orbit from the clarity she now sees.

"He is praying to me, Libra. He is praying to me!"

"Need I ask, what does he pray for, Moon?" Libra grows impatient.

"Here, I will allow you to listen."

With that, she casts a tunnel of sound over to Libra, her fellow neighbor, allowing him to hear the humble words of the Lone Wolf. The signal wavers in and out for a brief moment but breaks through just in time for Libra to hear his words and their message.

"Dear Moon, I know you're up there. I see you every evening, night after night. You watch over me and I can feel your presence. I know I can. First, I want to say that I've been having a hard time lately. A real hard time. At this point, I don't know what the hell is happening to me anymore. I'm about to give up. For many years, I haven't felt like myself. Look at this body of mine. It's sick. Do you see it? Completely frail, weak, and thin. I'm too young to experience this. I have dreams and visions, expectations and goals, and they have all been crushed under the weight of this illness. Whatever malady I have, because the doctors don't even know.

"I've tried everything under the sun to heal it, but clearly nothing's worked, not even the removal of my gallbladder. Screw them. They convinced me to have it removed and I still bellow in pain, losing weight by the minute."

The Lone Wolf looks down and puts his right hand over the still palpable scar.

"I'm wasting away, physically and mentally. I'm hurting. I've lost my gardening job. My weakness was too much, and

I had no choice but to quit. I don't have the energy to see my friends, to skate, or make music. They ask me what's up. I ignore them; I don't want them to see my pain, my weakness, or my flaws."

It's true what he says. His shirt hangs loosely over his thin frame and whips like a flag on the windy hill where he kneels. Like many other Americans, he has been mysteriously sick for the whole bout of his twenties, the doctors unable to diagnose or cure his sufferings. What a young and healthy twenty-five-year-old man should never experience was everything the Lone Wolf experienced and more.

Life up until the sickness had treated him well. He had the mind of an artist, preferring to stay in solitude while reading and writing. He held a steady job which provided him a great knowledge of plants and a loyal group of friends. The sickness came on rapidly and suddenly, leaving him hunched over in pain one day to never again return to a normal life. The doctors scratched their heads and, well, you heard...

They even removed his gallbladder!

The Moon hears this, her heart captivated by what she did not know before. A silver teardrop sheds as she listens intently to his continuing prayer.

"I want to start over, Moon. I just don't know how, or what to do. The essence has been sucked out of me, and my soul is dying along with my body. I feel if this doesn't end soon... then...my life will."

There is a silence so long, the Moon worries her role will shift and the sun will replace her in the sky.

"I ask for your help, Moon. Please, hear the humbleness of my words, the pain of my expression. I share them in solitude with you and no one else. They come from my heart and the desire to heal my life."

He exhales in pain.

"Can you help me find a way out of this dull city, out of this depression, and better yet, out of this sickness? I need color and vitality, a place where I can be creative once again. I need guidance."

With that, the Lone Wolf lifts up two wildflowers he plucked from the ground and offers them to the Moon high above, uniting them with his now free-flying words.

"Ahhhhh!" the Moon wails such a sound that it shakes the solar system all the way to Scorpius in the southern celestial hemisphere.

"Everything alright over there?" Scorpius asks inadvertently from over eight hundred light-years away.

"Yes. Everything is fine. Moon is just having a...moment," Libra howls back, a rather sharp attitude on his tongue.

The conversation between Moon and Libra continues once more, with Libra guiding the way, granting permission for Moon to approve the Lone Wolf's plea.

"Here is what we shall do. Listen carefully, Moon," Libra starts. "You see that tiny little spec in the middle of the Pacific?"

"No, I don't."

"Hawaii, Moon! Hawaii!"

"Oh! I am just now starting to see it," Moon answers as the sun sets over the Kona coast.

"Great. Let's make this simple. Send the Lone Wolf to Hawaii. He is being summoned there by his astrological chart; with its transitioning attributes and all that fancy stuff. He's called to continue his life and well-being over there. You need not worry of the details, Moon, for it will be I who locates a community to take him in and support him in the years to come. All you need to do is light the way for him.

You know, Moon, just shine your light on him and propel him out to that floating rock—understood?"

Moon bows with utmost respect before flashing a luminous light, invisible to the human eye, down toward the Lone Wolf.

***

Before he leaves the grassy knoll behind, the Lone Wolf bends down to pluck another flower. He observes it and notices that this one already holds a sprinkling of dew.

"I want to experience something different. I'm ready."

He picks up his skateboard and walks over the hilltop when his attention is grabbed by a sudden wavering vision. It first appears as the image of a dolphin, until a distant memory gradually reveals itself. The memory he recalls is of a coworker from his past jobsite. The coworker had once told the Lone Wolf about wonderful story after he had returned from his trip to Hawaii.

"We swam with freakin' dolphins, bro! They were like right in front of my eyes, like I could almost touch them," his coworker barked while stocking the shelves.

Upon remembering this conversation while now on the hill, the Lone Wolf tilts his head as if this coworker is still talking to him from many months ago, but he just now happened to hear what was being said.

"Huh."

For the first time in ages the Lone Wolf, rather uplifted, smiles an authentic smile of joy at the idea of *Hawaii*.

ONCE UPON
A FULL MOON

———

The tall palms tower over me, casting their leafy shadow over the long, dark road. Hanging throughout their leaves are blue LED lights flashing, flashing, flashing from the jungle property beyond.

My attention is taken to the cars, most of them beaters topped with surfboard racks and "Aina" bumper stickers.[1] They make an even line up the entire right side of the road, bumper to bumper, awaiting their owners to rev 'em up once more. I hear music in the distance; its pulsation vibrates the ground from somewhere I cannot yet see. The location of this evening's gathering is situated just behind the foliage of Hawaii's thick jungle.

Adrenaline and excitement combine in my veins, creating a symphony like casual chaos, sparking an electric pulse I wasn't aware existed within me until now. I fall victim to a suave smile as I nod my head to the strong bass, already

———

1   A Hawaiian word that refers to "The Land" which we live on.

matching the energy of the party. My nerves quiver with amplification, creating a sensation of wanting to rush, wanting to push forward. The full moon casts her clear mercury light above my crown and onto the outline of my young and naive face. Right now, I am younger than I know, more inexperienced than I wish, and walk with more courage than I could even understand.

Approaching the gate, I see smiling faces lit by the smoky shadows of fire torches. They wear a mask of jaded glory as they notice the stupid smile lining my face. My dress hovers over the barren ground, occasionally contacting with the rocky terrain I stand upon. Its long pink fabric covers my body like a colorful veil, concealing my earnest nature. My bronzed skin shows just how well Hawaii has been treating me, matching the sublime highlights that shimmer throughout my hair.

A drink moistens my lips. I often try to avoid such daring luxuries, but tonight my faultless ego gives permission. Nervous pulses fluctuate throughout my body as I force myself to belong here and now. Everyone at this party seems to be from the same tribe, at least for tonight. After this, we will all part ways and forget this moment ever existed. This is how we gather down here in South Kona.

In the courtyard people are everywhere, as they usually are. The local band works their instruments with force, echoing their vibrations from the garage. I can almost feel the heart of the guitarist, pulsing in tandem with the audience he enchants before him. Mango trees hang loosely over the scene, offering a gentle reminder of our good fortune of living on an island. The dancing girls are free-moving, their muscles as relaxed as their lifestyles. The men are potent with drinks in their hands, targets in their eyes, and exotic thoughts in their minds.

I'm not sure if I know anyone here. It's even safe to say I still don't know my own self. Toward the house, I happen to notice someone with a slightly recognizable face. He stands firm, joint in mouth, at the entrance. He is the slob of a dude I met a few weeks back while visiting a local beach. Behind him is a makeshift bar elegantly propped up, two strong men serving drinks. I walk toward this scene as embarrassment follows closely behind, shyness whispering in my footsteps. Greeting the familiar face, I stand around making small talk with him—very small talk. Constant glances over my shoulder highlight my disinterest in this unassuming conversation.

"How did you arrive here?" He tries to maintain my attention.

"Hitched a ride and got dropped off." I speak with too much effort just to get my voice through the music.

"Looking good." He gives me a look. "You're in the right—"

His words don't matter.

Nothing matters anymore.

I've gone momentarily deaf and blind to everything except to an essence of light that I've never seen before.

With my ears muted, my sight dials in on this target: a slender figure who walks through the gate, arriving in the courtyard. The same courtyard I'm in. Time stops and stands on a pedestal so mighty, that I lose any and every recognition of my life, who I am, where am I, and so on. What my vision witnesses is amplified like a peek through a magnifying glass. Propelling itself from the center of my chest, my heart now beats faster than those flashing blue LED lights.

Clearly, I don't know him. His frame is slender and sleek, tall, and lean. His skin glistens like the sand of the high desert, a golden-brown mirage, enticing me like nectar. His hair is thick, with waves more perfect than any the Pacific Ocean could conceive. He walks with a stride I already seem to be familiarized with.

But who the *hell* is he?

I can't refrain from gawking, from absorbing the fine details of his actions, mannerisms, and expressions. I feel like I know him, but I certainly don't. I've never experienced trickery such as this before. What I'm experiencing now is more than attraction. I'm convinced of it. It's something karmic and cosmic, leaving me mesmerized and stupid.

I'm still in a trance of pure lust, drooling over this handsome young fellow. My eyes don't dare turn away from the light he casts with every beckoning step toward me.

Nearer to me.

Closer to me.

In front of me.

I have a mid-moment explosion in my mind before I register that his hand is being held out to me, awaiting mine to meet his.

Reality breaks fast as I fall out of my stupor and become aware of my surroundings.

He is still waiting for my reciprocation.

In an instant everything changes, for his hand is now holding mine and I am holding his.

I am holding his hand.

He is touching me.

I am touching him.

The moment lasts forever but ends just in time.

Just in time for me to make a fool out of myself.

"What's your name?"

There's a small pause as the situation waits for my naive display.

"My name is Deanna."

He is speaking to me, but I don't hear him.

I can't because the music is way too loud.

All I know is his name starts with a J. Is it *Jeremey*? *Jean*?

Whatever, who cares? All that matters to me right now are the words tumbling out of my still gaping mouth.

"You're beautiful."

I can't act, move, or speak of anything else.

Just those two words.

Then it comes again, as if once wasn't enough.

"You're beautiful."

Before I know it, his hand is no longer in mine, and he is walking back out into the midst of the crowd.

Did he even hear me?

Should I have said it a *third* time?

***

"I need to get to know him."

I look at the sloppy dude from before who is still puffing on his joint. I say these words aloud, not necessarily for him but for myself.

I don't care of the Fool I have made of myself.

I don't care at all.

I'm on a mission to find the man I am newly enamored with.

"I really need to get to know him," I confirm.

"Oh, yeah. That guy? He's a cool guy," the slob responds in nonchalance.

Acting slightly from desire but more from instinct, the same karmic force pulls me into an altered state of being, casting me into a trance of what I presume is love. I believe they call it "love at first sight."

I walk further into the courtyard, my vision active like a hawk. I look for him, keeping my eyes wide. I have absolutely nothing planned to say when I do see him. I've already said it all. I just want to see him and his beautiful face once more. I cruise my way throughout the entire lively compound—the kitchen, the courtyard, the bar. Goddamn, I even check the trampoline and the treehouse.

I don't see him anywhere.

Maybe he was an angel, coming to tease me like this.

In my search, I observe and record every other guest gathered here tonight, dressed in their unique garb, showing off their curves and creativity. Each person is so exquisite. My brain curb stomps my heart and I become aware of an insecurity—a desire to stand out among the crowd so that he will notice me and only me.

In semi-defeat, I make my way to the tranquil gardens out back. Perched among a large stone, I breath myself into my body. My heart palpitates like a crazy bat, fluttering around with one quest in mind. I see my foolish ways for what they are, but that doesn't lessen the obsession inside of me. Not at all. In fact, the obsession grows grander, seemingly out of reach. An obsession I must grasp onto, but cannot even see with my own eyes.

My attention is pulled down below as a path beyond where I perch reveals itself. I walk ahead in hesitance, nearly blind to what lies before me in the dim lighting. The setting is mysterious; invisible ferns brush past my ankles, frogs, and critters deepen their echo. No one is around me here.

I am alone.

I inquire to myself for an authentic display of advice:

How can I get his attention when I see him next?

Be confident. That's it. Be bold. Be yourself.

It's the only answer I summon.

Okay, well, easier said than done.

I swallow my resistance and go for gold.

Or better yet, the dance floor.

***

Through the thundering music of the live band and the pool of bodies moving to the bass, I find my way toward the stage and let my inner demons range free. The obsessive search barrels off my chest, falling away from me. I swirl and twirl like all the other hippie girls among me, hair moving as I lift up one side of my dress. I hear the trumpet chant and people cheer. A beer is handed to me. I dance with caution so as not to spill it.

My hair gets wilder by the minute, curling and knotting with each drop of sweat. It falls in front of my face, covering my eyesight and taking me away with the sounds of the band that brings us alive tonight.

My eyes are closed. I swirl.

My eyes are open. I twirl.

My eyes are closed. I turn forward.

My eyes are open. I turn backward.

His eyes are closed. He twirls.

His eyes are open. He swirls.

His eyes are closed. He turns backward.

His eyes are open. He turns forward.

Our eyes are open.

Time stands still as the sea of bodies between us divinely part right down the middle, letting god and goddess through. His long arms stretch out toward me. I accept the cue and sync up to his rhythm and pace. My arms mimic his; I take his hands in mine, different than before. Certainly different than before. We're facing one another, smiles on our faces.

I know for a fact we had both been looking for each other. Not just at this party, but in this lifetime.

He twirls me around.

I abide.

He swirls around me.

I allow.

We move faster to the rising beat, matching our footsteps, entangling our energy.

Which direction is up, and which direction is down?

We're in a whirling frenzy, and I don't care to ever stop.

"I like the way you move," his voice greets me with the same playfulness.

"Let's head outside."

I agree.

I follow his lead as he grabs for my hand and leads me through the same jungle maze out back, under the moonlight and through the ferns. We weave in and out of a labyrinth of people, arriving at the mysterious garden once more. No longer am I alone. I have received my wish. We find a private space, sitting side by side on a step made from lava rock, a graceful conversation already being birthed.

"What brought you to the island? I haven't seen you around before."

"Well, I left my home in Jersey a few months back. My intentions had been to stay on a farm, learn the lifestyle, do some farming, and that's exactly what I did. I've been living at a place in Kealakekua, picking coffee and macadamia nuts. Being out here is a dream for a suburban girl like me. How about yourself? Are you from here?"

"No, I'm not. I'm originally from Utah, Salt Lake City. To be honest, my story is quite personal. I'm not so sure I made the decision to come out here. I like to say the island called me out here." He stops his thoughts and brings his face up toward the night sky, with its glistening stars and full moon. "Being out here saved my life. It's been a sanctuary for me, a place of purity. Anyway, let's not get into that. Do you practice yoga?"

He stops himself short directly at the spot where I'm yearning to know more. I don't push. I allow the conversation to happen as it does, not wanting to impose by inquiring further about his seemingly odd past.

"I do. I just started practicing a few months back. What *really* interests me, though, is Ayurveda. Do you know what that is, the natural healing system of India?"

A smile like a crescent moon rises upon his face.

"I knew there was a reason why I liked you. Ayurveda has been my backbone for healing. I always assumed not many others know about it."

A man who knows about Ayurveda?

Get out. Ever since I've learned about the ancient healing arts, I haven't been able to keep my curiosity away from it. The herbs, the tonics, the massages, the philosophies—every part of it intrigues me.

Our eyes lock. I'm in awe.

My trance is still in play.

Our karmic destiny finally happening.

His face nears mine. I can smell his salty skin. His lips meet mine. I can taste the salt through his kiss.

Just as my body leans in closer to his, he pulls away, halting the production.

"Let's go back to my place."

I grab his hand as he towers over me and pulls me onto my feet, following behind him once again. Under the moonlight and out of the party we stroll, passing by the roaring cacophony like a hovering cloud. Past the dense trees, where mysterious noises emanate. Past the long row of beat-up island cruisers.

Until we arrive at a lone, laughable, silver scooter.

"Hop on."

I grab below my knees, lifting my long pink dress, the one with the white floral design embedded around the curves of my breasts, and I ride off with him.

To where?

I have no idea.

I just hold on tight to the handsome man who controls my destiny. We make our way up the obscure, winding road. The wind whips through my hair, making me feel all the freer. My thoughts are silenced now, both by the loud hum of the motor and the simmering content inside of me. As the towering trees pass us, I press my face into his back and breathe him in. His presence upon me is so new, yet so familiar.

It feels like I've been breathing him in forever.

Air.

THE DIRTY SHACK

———

We arrive.

Or so I *think*.

I don't see any type of housing structure on the property yet.

Air props his scooter up, positioning it alongside the tall cane grass, then he comes at me and grabs my hand, leading me up a steep hill.

"Watch your step."

Walking hand-in-hand, he lures me up the hill. I'm in such a state of enchantment I don't notice the ramshackle structure towering over us until we arrive at a random set of stairs casted in cement. I glance down intending to only watch my step, but my eye is caught by a few words fastened into the cement, written in small stones: "The Dirty Shack."

"Here we are."

My brain falters for a second. Who would name a home that?

What's so dirty about living in the jungle?

Climbing over the steps, I follow Air through the open door of the shack.

Here and now is where I quickly discover my answer.

Yes. It is a dirty shack indeed.

Or a whacky shack, a creative shack.

Let's agree on one thing: it's definitely a shack. A coffee shack, that is, complete with aged tin panels that construct the roof. It looks more like a proper structure on the inside than on the outside. Built with large wooden makeshift panels, the outside just gives a unique structure to the rooms inside.

I'm in awe. My eyes take their sweet time adjusting to the lackluster lighting inside. A dim glow emits from a single light suspended from a hole in the roof. Even at my youthful age, it takes a fine moment to bring my senses up to par.

Where am I?

Of course, I'm in the kitchen. Complete with a sink, shelves, rusted stovetop, and all. Above the stove rests a long flimsy shelf where fifteen spice jars perch, simulating an image of birds gathered upon a telephone wire. My eyes cast downward and I nearly chuckle aloud as I see the red-and-white-tiled paint of the floor that I stand upon, speckled at best with dust, dirt, and debris. I'm reminded of a circus. A sudden shadow scatters into a hidden corner—a cockroach. I ignore the sight and continue forward, noticing Air is no longer in the kitchen with me.

Lurching further into the depths of this shack, I pass by aged walls, colorful and flamboyant. They match the walls of my once-teenage bedroom: bright greens, reds, yellows, and oranges. Each seemingly "pop-up" wall has its own charismatic appeal. One wall hosts a series of paintings—abstract art in dusty frames. Another wall reveals a large green door with a magnificent doorknob and lock, giving off an *Alice in Wonderland* vibe.

I pass over a small wooden step and enter what I believe to be the dining room of this funhouse. My handsome admirer is still nowhere to be found. My curiosity is grabbed again, this time by the sight of a long and dusty bookshelf beyond the dining room table. Even from this far away, I can see the shelf is efficiently guarded by cobwebs of all shapes and sizes. I have a hard time reading any of the titles.

Oh well.

Contained in the dining room is a bulky round table taking up most of the space. It has a clear layer of shellac, for beneath it is the depiction of a bizarre face with a Caribbean flair. I feel the face staring at me as I walk past it, like an idle guard watching over its clock tower.

Without stopping, my body automatically arrives at the furthest and final room of the Dirty Shack. Well, it's a room, but a room without walls. There are only half panels and the upper portion is completely open. It exposes me to the cooling breeze of the night.

Walking over to the edge, I set my face toward the breeze. In my gleeful stupor, I don't notice anything else around me. This Dirty Shack is a dream—my dream. Every new-age hippie's delight. Its quirkiness, its potential to collapse at any moment, its colors. How perfect could it be that the most unique man I've ever met lives in the most unique housing I've ever stood in? I'm the creator of this dream, the weaver of this web, barely able to believe this is happening.

I rest my chin over the ledge and count the stars above. About to drift away into the night sky, I am gently called back to my body through the soft sound of a piano.

***

There he is, long, tan and handsome, with his frame arching over the elegant instrument. One by one the keys are touched by the tips of his fingers, creating an endearing melody that summons me from the ledge where I stand. I walk over to his side and join him on the bench. I take a seat and slide my arm around his thin waist, bringing my face to nuzzle his shoulder.

He is already mine.

His anthem sets the mood for this moment, giving me another reason to be entranced. I lose myself as he performs for me and only me. The vibrations from the keys are soothing; they lull me into faraway galaxies, sacred places, and an arousal of freedom.

It's incredible, to be this young.

The pace of his song slows down, a signal for me to reestablish my thoughts and come to reality. He pulls away from the last key, the sound emanating into a fade. Taking my face into his hands, he kisses me softly, once, twice, three times, before he stands up to leave the room, beckoning me to follow.

"I'll make some tea for us."

I tiptoe behind him as he stops in the rustic kitchen, grabbing a kettle and two small, stained mugs.

"This is just the main house. I still need to show you where I live."

***

We arrive at the base of a steep wooden ladder where Air makes his way up first, calling out behind me to wait "just a moment."

He disappears, leaving me in my own abyss of questions and wonderment. My head is tilted upward, and my eyes do not leave the small opening from which he vanished. I hear him walking around in the loft, tinkering with something, until my waiting is finally made clear.

An array of Christmas lights flash on instantly, wrapping themselves around the two-story structure to light the way up the ladder and set the ambiance for my entry. His head peeks from behind two thin curtains hanging just over the last step.

"Okay, you can come up now. Just watch your step. These stairs are tricky."

I lift up my long dress once again, one hand grabbing the fabric and the other clutching onto the wooden steps. One by one I make my way up until I arrive near the top. He doesn't hesitate to take my hand, pulling me up and into this magical loft perched high atop the canopies.

"Welcome to my sanctuary. I call it 'the pagoda.'"

"Woah. This is where you live?" My head circles around the entire majestic space, absorbing it all in one gulp.

The rustic wooden desk houses his speakers, computer, and microphone. Long, cream-colored curtains hang in place of walls. There is a full-size bed, fitting just so, in the corner, next to a small bookshelf full of books that emphasize yoga or Ayurveda. I notice the continuation of the Christmas lights, how they coil themselves around the upper wooden frame of the room, as the only source of light.

"Girl, I've been living here for a few years now."

I'm starting to feel like Princess Jasmine, taken away on a magic carpet (or scooter) ride and ending up in a hidden rustic space, filled with an essence I can't put my finger on, yet one which also feels strangely familiar.

"I can't believe this. You live in such a beautiful spot. It's unique. I've truly never seen anything like this before."

Air presses a button on his computer, dials in the speakers, and begins the soundtrack for tonight: chill-vibe jazz with a little extra bass.

He walks over to me, pushing my hair aside.

"I can't believe it, either. You're so beautiful, so unique, like nothing I've ever seen before."

Our gazes meet, not breaking until he invites me to take a seat on the small brown couch.

"Get cozy."

I obey, getting myself even more comfortable. Leaning forward to grab my mug of tea off the coffee table, I make sure not to take my eyes off him. I continue to examine his every move. He is swift and soft, aware of his steps. He still strikes me as a familiar presence, but if I've met him before my brain cannot locate the memory file. His grace is delicate as if he's floating, drifting on over to the couch and right alongside me.

"So..."

His deep amber eyes meet mine.

"Did you see it?" His voice is faint, brushing by me like a swift breeze.

"See what?"

"The moon. Did you see the moon?"

Oh, right. He is referring to tonight's moon, the December Wolf Moon.

"Of course I did. How could I miss a full moon on a night like tonight?"

"Well, that just makes this coincidence all the better. I was referring to the moon on the ceiling of this pagoda."

His head tilts upward, guiding me to do the same.

"Oh. Wow."

Right smack in the middle of the roof, like an unfolding lotus, a thick wooden circle presents itself. It's painted in an indigo blue and decorated with swirls and specs, depicting a full and feminine moon.

"The roof is my favorite part about this space. That moon above us symbolizes so much for me. I've always been a lover of the night; it makes me feel mysterious. While I was living in Salt Lake City, before I got sick, I spent countless evenings cruising the streets. Everywhere I went would be vacant, devoid of cars, devoid of humans. There was something about that—the emptiness, the stillness—that made me feel alive."

I nod my head, his words coming to life in my mind.

"I see this room as having a connection to the moon, its phases, and its lure of creativity. As an artist, I pride myself on those qualities, not to mention the profound healing I've found through it. The moon, along with this island and my yoga practice, has nurtured me to a state of better health."

He speaks with a confident vulnerability. I've never heard a man say such detailed and lovely things. My karmic tie to this person in front of me is whole and untethered. I am full like the moon herself.

"I agree. I've been learning more about her cycles and how they play a powerful role in our lives, whether we are conscious of it or not. The energy of a full moon influences our moods, appetite, and the fruition of our goals or projects. There *is* something so enchanting about her; she is a portal into the unknown."

The soothing jazz music pours out its rhythm, filling the spaces of silence that follow my words. He doesn't respond to what I say. He just stares at me. I glance down shyly, hands wrapped around my teacup, taking a sip.

His soft voice gently breaks the silence.

"I enjoy being around you. I feel very comfortable."

I blush.

"I can say the same about you."

Side by side we sit and sip our herbal teas, delving further into conversations about astrology, yoga, and life itself. If any anxieties arise within me, they dissipate just as quickly. His presence is warm and welcoming, making me feel invited as he doesn't force himself on me in the way men typically do, but talks with me and listens to me.

It's as if a deep trust has formed before this evening ever took place.

It's as if we have been summoned together by the essence of the island.

We finish the last few sips of our lukewarm tea, moving our bodies closer toward each other like opposing magnets.

I press my entire body into his graceful embrace. His fluttering heart goes off and I listen to it. All the stories this heart has experienced—I want to hear them all. He spoke a few times of an illness he encountered; I want to know about it. I close my eyes and listen intently to his heartbeat and the rhythm of his pacifying breath. He holds me tight as we both drift off into the astral realm.

***

Would you believe in love at first sight now if I told you that before this I hadn't either? I'm romantic, yes, but not a softie. If someone would've asked me prior to this enchanted evening what I thought about love at first sight, I would've given it to them straight. I would've gotten all New Jersey on them and told them that attraction takes time to build, you idiot, and trust takes years. I'd go on to back it up by commenting that such forces of nature are unreal and lustful. I was never one for Disney—no, no, no. I like the real stuff, not the whimsical, fairytale, romance novel shove-it-up-your-ass junk.

But what am I to do now, finding myself in the center of this conundrum?

Uh, go with it I guess.

It's so much better when you're on the inside, anyway.

A glance over my shoulder at just the perfect moment has now led me to believe that coincidence is karma's weaker brother.

You see, I also did not believe in the destiny of karma until those two hands were offered to me on the dance floor. The synchronistic events that followed our small talk in the garden revealed two things:

1. Nothing is planned.
2. Everything is predestined.

As we sat high atop in the pagoda during the night of the full moon, gazing up at the flawless ceiling all while falling in love, I realized that life has a twisted way of working things out. We exist in between what we "plan" for ourselves and the events that are predestined for us.

I planned to stay in Hawaii for three months.

Just three months.

Plane ticket purchased and all.

And whoever destined for me to meet my soulmate four days before my departure is an *asshole*.

For four days straight I was thrust back and forth, like the waning and waxing of the moon herself, into a state of ecstasy alongside Air and into a state of heartache.

Four days with your soulmate is equivalent to a lifetime.

Yet a lifetime spent with your soulmate is equivalent to four days.

Do you see the irony here?

How am I to say goodbye after waking up our first morning together and rolling out our yoga mats alongside each other?

How am I to say goodbye after meeting all of his seven (or eleven, I forget) housemates at the Dirty Shack and coming to admire every one of them?

Especially, how am I to say goodbye to a man with thick, curly hair and deep amber eyes who refers to me as his *Pele's Moonlight*?

If you don't know who Pele is, she's the fierce Hawaiian goddess of passion, creation, and destruction.

Just to put things into context.

Do you see, now, why I am ailed?

How often does one happen upon a fantasy such as this?

My final hours of being here in Hawaii, and I spend them inside my meager tent, packing my suitcase and wondering such things. I'll have a whole twelve-hour flight, which I'm very much resisting, to continue this tortuous contemplation.

ISLAND QUEEN

The plane swoops low over the drab buildings and ominous sky as it lands. I get off, dazed and confused, making my way to the baggage claim. It isn't until I camouflage with the daunting presence of Newark that I notice my heart hasn't made the journey back with me. I roll my luggage over and take a seat atop it, slouched like a grump while waiting for my father to pick me up. My entertainment comes from the frantic movements and jerks of the frenzied people of New Jersey. Their serious faces hang nearly as low as the grey clouds outside.

Damn.

Could the contrast between these two places be any more drastic?

As my plane had taken off in Hawaii, the indigo blue ocean and spring green palm fronds taunted me from below, a gentle torture, reminding me I was about to leave this life behind. I said goodbye to Air at the front of the airport, sealing our romance with a kiss and a salty tear.

My father finally arrives, a hint of excitement on his face, but my shoulders can't help but hang low. He curses and swerves his way through the turnpike traffic, amusing me and taking my mind somewhat off the memories that race like shooting stars through my mind. The ones keeping me stuck in this moonlight fantasy.

Dreary days tumble on lifelessly, as I gear up for the holidays. I'm a sad Fool, a very sad Fool. Sinister, frustrated, and hurt, I lash out at my family, delivering my pains onto them and inappropriately attributing my misfortune to them. If my life had once depicted a spectacularly colored photograph, all the color has now been drained out, leaving behind a grey film completely indecipherable and void of emotion.

I've spent countless days in my room, sleeping long hours like a cat and blaming it on the jet lag. I've avoided my mother at all costs, timing my meals in between her comings and goings. Here I am once more: the middle child, misunderstood and underrated. I keep to myself because, well, that's what middle children do. We are the reason the family portrait never hangs straight. We are the least acknowledged, yet tend to be the most disappointing, which doesn't make sense at all. Forget black sheep—we are the black dragons, resembling somewhat of a mystical creature, wondering if we really exist.

***

I pull the black t-shirt over my head, letting it fall above my bleached white pants. It's a wonder my old job took me back after the way I walked out on them before. I suppose I never took the time to burn my bridges fully. I dislike this job—scooping ice cream for all of Brick—but it's the only job I've ever known, and I don't have anything better to do with myself after arriving in Jersey during the middle of winter.

It's been a drag, to say the least. A long, painful, and blistering drag. I thought my life would be different now, forever altered, never to return to this small suburban town. But only idiots insist on such things.

I walk toward the mirror while braiding my hair. Here comes my reflection. Two open and empty eyes from where my hope has been siphoned glare back at me. My once bronzed skin from the Hawaiian sun has completely faded into a pale hue, matching the grey semblance just outside my windows.

Why did I agree to get on that plane? I shudder at the sadness still present inside of me and I toss my braid over my shoulder. After what I experienced in Hawaii, how could I return to this lackluster life? I had intended to make a promise to myself, a promise to never return here. My naivety embarrasses me, and for that I am even more resentful.

No community potlucks.

No ripe papaya.

No Air.

I can hardly breathe without him.

I'm not being dramatic.

I'm being honest.

I can't go a minute without thinking of the dude. I told you this was some karmic shit. I'm just not sure if it's the good kind or bad kind, if there even is such a thing. My admiration toward him is a spellbound obsession. I ponder frequently about the secrets he shared, clutching them inside me like a witch who has stolen a secret ingredient. What am I going to do with these things?

Nothing, aside from think about them over and over.

That's what "love" does to you.

It makes you feral.

It makes you an animal.

It makes you sick.

I know. I know.

I've been a damn fool.

I'll swallow the pill now and focus on the life I detest in New Jersey.

I pack my lunch for tonight's shift, a lousy meal if I may, anything to keep me away from those gummy bears. Hey, remember that big round table I told you about at the Dirty Shack? You should have seen the meals served on that thing— Thai noodles, Indian curries, pizzas. I hate to say it, I really do, but they were all...*vegan*.

Accommodating everyone's sensitivities and generating no complaints.

A feat I wouldn't see for a million years in the Amodeo residence.

Despite my ongoing obsession with Air, he did teach me something worthwhile, and that was the mere initiation of preparing and cooking food. No recipe, no guides, just taste buds and trust. I liked everything he made me. Before I left, he gifted me a masala box: a round, stainless-steel container with small cups which separate the different herbs and spices typically used in Indian dishes. We stopped at the market, purchasing from the bulk section fennel seeds, turmeric, cloves, coriander, cumin, and curry powder.

I've been using them each day as I practice my skills of preparation and flavor combination. This has sent my Sicilian mother and father into a fit, as they have never even laid eyes on turmeric until now. Cumin seeds? Forget about it; they almost cried upon smelling them while they cooked. Each time I use the spices, my father comes running into the kitchen.

"What the hell is that smell? What's going on in here?"

When he sees the pan sizzling, he responds by immediately removing himself from the kitchen while fanning the air.

It's hilarious.

Because it happens *every time*.

I guess I could say I enjoy being in Jersey a little bit.

***

I lay down on the narrow frame of my childhood bed. Work tonight was exhausting and my legs are throbbing. I couldn't even resist those gummy bears. Damnit, they get me every time. Rolling over on my bed, a vision thrusts itself into my mind. Different than a memory, this vision has potential—a message. It speaks to me in the hushed voice of a female.

"You will go back."

I push down the sensation, avoiding the torture, and reach for my phone.

It lights up, casting its screen straight into my pupils and its notifications into my...*pounding heartbeat*.

Two missed calls.

One text.

"Dee, call me back."

Oh shit. Oh shit.

I sit up, exhaustion vanishing.

I inhale deeply, if only to inflate my mood, and do as he says.

I call him back.

He answers first ring.

"What's up?"

I smile.

"How are you?"

"Good. I'm over here at the shack, and we're making tacos tonight. I'm calling to invite you over."

Damn him. That jerk knows I wish I could be there.

"Ah. If I do come I'll be a bit late. Save me some?"

"For sure. You got the hot sauce?"

"Cholula."

"Chee! You got it, girl."

I exhale loudly, a laugh under my breath.

My longing to join him creates a black hole in my heart.

"So...When are you coming?"

My heart jumps.

"When do you want me to come?"

He hoots into the phone playfully.

"Girl, I want you to come here *right now*. I miss you, Sweet Dee."

Am I tripping?

"If you want me to come back, I will. Don't tempt me."

"Then do it. I want to see you again."

Oh. He isn't kidding.

"How about I come when my semester ends?"

"Well, these tacos won't be good by then, but you're always welcome here in my nest."

He's hilarious.

"So, you're down? I'm not joking."

"As long as you want it to be, but it has to be on two conditions."

Even though his voice is suave, my muscles tighten.

"Oh yeah? What's that?"

"The first is that you don't forget the Cholula."

He pauses, his voice turning sweeter.

"And the second is that you be my island queen. I'm ready to commit to you, Dee. Will you be my girl?"

Well, what a surprise. His girl? It took him two months to call and ask me this? Maybe he had to miss me a little. You know how guys are, or maybe you don't. But guys like to miss things, especially pretty little things.

Anyway, I'm on cloud nine over here. Of course, I'll be his girl. Did you not hear me wailing on just moments prior? Red flags? Psh. Those are just suggestions. What's more important is the mercury running through my veins. It's activated the drug of his attention once more. I'm floating. No, I'm *free*-falling.

"Your girl, huh? Sure. You got me. Can't make any promises on the Cholula, though."

His laughter passes through the phone, filling me up with a breath of fresh air.

***

She slides the cards across the table. I take in the crisscross pattern garnishing their backside. Seventy-eight cards in total, from which I select ten. This is my first encounter with the tarot deck, though my interest in it has been long withstanding. I crave to know more about my upcoming journey, and of course that silly little relationship I've got going. I close my eyes and set my intentions, desperately hoping to hear all I know to be true.

Sitting across from the reader, I begin to feel an odd yet secure connection to her. We are opposites in our age, our hair, and our fashion. Her glowing pale skin opposes my bronzed Mediterranean skin. Her green eyes contrast against my brown eyes. Her casual wear makes me look even more bohemian.

"Okay, they're ready. Go ahead and pick ten cards with your left hand." Her thick Staten Island accent adds further to this authentic moment.

My left hand anxiously reaches across the glass table.

1...2

...3...4...5

..6...7...

...8...9...

...10...

I pick them out, one by one, then watch as Eileen places the rest of the deck off to the side.

She slows down her movements and stares at the un-flipped cards I have chosen.

The sacred ten.

Her arm moves gracefully across the table. As her hand contacts each card, she flips it with a peculiar reluctance, exposing its awaiting message. They are in place, aligned, and observed. Now I wait.

And I wait...

...And wait.

She doesn't speak just yet, but keeps her eyes cast downward while the cards glare upward toward her. The anticipation seizes me, wrapping itself around my throat like a snake. The large clock on the wall ticking loudly.

I stop breathing.

"Okay," she finally conjures, "so, what these cards are saying to me is that you're going on a trip, a voyage. That's what this Three of Wands here represents. You are traveling somewhere far or overseas. It's going to be a good journey, and I can see you're ready for it."

She taps on the top card.

"But you're very nervous about going. You don't know what to expect and you aren't sure about the details of how it will pan out—Nine of Swords. I see a lot of anxiety."

She exhales forcefully, as if matching the density of this card.

"Your father is worried for you. I see him popping up twice in this reading, over here with the Emperor card and down here with the Death card in reverse."

I nod my head in alliance.

"Yeah, that makes sense."

"Your father doesn't want you to go, you know that?"

"I do."

"But I do see you going on the trip. You may have some challenges arising, but the Eight of Cups tells me you're leaving everything from your past behind to take this journey."

She waits before focusing her gaze on the next card, her face silently sighing. What she says next really knocks the breath out of me.

"Are you in a relationship?"

"Yeah, I am, but it's long distance."

She nods, opens her mouth to relay something, but halts herself and changes her words.

"And you are going to see him on this trip?"

"Yeah. I'm moving back to Hawaii to be with him."

The clock ticks and my heart races. I begin to sweat profusely.

What can she see? I must know *now*.

Anxious and on defense, I can't wait a moment longer.

"What do you see?"

She speaks slow and clear.

"Okay, I see here..." she pauses. "I see here, Deanna, that there is love between you two, hence the Lovers card, but with this Three of Swords card I can see something dishonest stands between you two. What I'm hearing is that he's not telling you everything."

She turns the Three of Swords card around so I can see its picture more clearly, but there is not much more to observe on this card. It shows one giant, lone-standing heart with three swords piercing through it.

She repeats its message again and places the card back in her pile.

"I keep getting that there is something he isn't telling you. I can't see what it's about, but just know that there is more to the story than he is willing to share."

My heart sinks.

I don't believe it.

I want to hear more, to deter my emotions.

She waits before moving on.

"I do see that you're going to learn a lot from him, with the Three of Pentacles right here. It's a card which reminds us how we learn from each other's levels of experience—an important aspect. There is certainly a bigger meaning behind your relationship, to grow and learn, but what the cards keep telling me Deanna, is that you two are star-crossed lovers."

I see it.

There in between the Lovers card and the Three of Swords sits a perfect little card in reverse: the Moon card. Its reversed state signifying an illusion, or deception, a fantasy.

The room is silent.

My heart nearly sacrifices its next beat.

I am *still* not breathing.

Her striking words ring through my head until they are broken by her actual voice.

"This last card here shows me that you truly don't mind taking risks—in travel, in romance, in opportunity. You're willing to learn with or without consequence. You're on a journey of learning and freedom. This is a great sign, this card."

She flips it around and shows it to me.

I take it in my hands.

"Oh, great. Now I'm the Fool?"

"Don't be so quick to judge. The Fool is the one who has the adventures, Deanna, and adventures typically lead to stories."

She takes the card back and clears the table, signifying her time here is complete.

I hear her voice again in my head later that night, completely disregarding everything else she mentioned except for:

"Star-crossed lovers."

"There is something he isn't telling you."

What is a star-crossed lover?

I want to ask her, but I already know.

What is he not telling me?

I want to ask him, but I already...

No...

***

"Ladies and gentlemen, you're flying today with Alaskan Airlines. We hope you—"

I block out the announcement with my earphones, focusing my attention instead on my precious daydreams of Hawaii life to come. I spent my final weeks in New Jersey sorting through the last of my unnecessary belongings and selling my clothes, jewelry, and trinkets. I made a point to visit each friend before parting ways. Who knows how long I will be gone this time?

My parents, who were very relieved upon my initial return, are now even more aggravated because I denied enrollment into Rutgers' food science program, officially dropping out of college for a third time.

"Charles, why would I study preserving food in a lab when I want to learn how to grow my own food from soil?" I had yelled across the kitchen at my father.

"I just don't know what you're gonna with your life."

"I'll figure it out."

No one understands my motive for these sudden changes in my life—the alteration of my diet, my desire to travel, living minimally, not attending university. But maybe it's just because I am finally becoming my own person, giving myself a chance to explore and learn. I'm going against the grain of everything I've ever been told.

"That's just not the way I want to do things," I explained to my mother.

"Well no one has ever won an award for being brave, Deanna."

My laughter had sent her out of the kitchen like the perfected repellant.

Now I will return to the land where I belong: the lush green canopies of Hawaii, the living soil made of lava, the home of Mauna Kea. Hawaii is a sacred place where many folks fantasize about living, but few get to experience its deeper charm. It's a spiritual gem that asks us to grow, not to mention one of the most isolated lands in the world.

An entire island that is alive, surrounded by water, active volcanos, trade winds, rainforests, deserts, and jungles.

Who would say no to a perfectly ripe mango?

Or papaya? Or apple banana? Or avocado?

Okay, you get the point.

Who would say no to food *not* grown in labs.

Just a month prior, Eileen had read my tarot cards and left me full of quiet anxieties that I've come to ignore so perfectly. I've been speaking with Air consistently, reigniting the same connection we had during our four precious days together. All the gracious words in the world cannot explain how it feels right now to finally be reunited with my beloved, my moonlight romance once again. I see his face in my mind with his soft and sweet eyes. I hear his voice, the subtle play of his humor, as I drift into an elated state, free-falling into his reality.

I am nearly asleep, relaxed, and soothed by the humming aircraft.

My eyes burst open, jolting me.

Shit.

I forgot the hot sauce.

VALLEY OF THE MOON

———

I arrive after sunset. The fourteen-hour flight settles in my eyes the same way dusk settles over the ocean. I'm half-asleep, yet my nerves still stir. I make my way to the restroom and change my clothes into a fresh and planned outfit. Women do these kinds of things; can you blame me? The humid air outside immediately makes my hair frizzy, reminding me that I'm finally home. The island is a quiet place, and from the open airport one can even hear the waves of the surrounding ocean rolling in.

What bliss.

Now where is he?

I only brought one carry-on with me, going minimal, ready to reset my life. It rolls obediently behind me, tracing the black pavement. I walk slowly, my eyes squinting from a combination of exhaustion and the dim lighting. I first lay my eyes on the jalopy, a long white Subaru with a surf rack on top, rusted frame, and tinted windows. It's parked half-assed alongside the curb.

Then I see him.

He exits the vehicle, hair as magnificent as I fantasized and skin just as bronzed as ever.

I collapse into his arms, laughing from the break of tension six thousand miles and six months created. My head is placed against his familiar chest, squeezing him tight and making up for all the time we spent in separation. I breathe him in as he embraces me, reacquainting myself with the salty scent of his skin. Every single day we spent apart dissipates with this one moment, this coming together in the same exact spot where we kissed and said our goodbyes half a year prior.

He cups my face in his hands, pushing aside my hair in that very sexy way.

"Welcome back, babe; you made it. How was the flight?"

"It was a long one, but I'm so stoked to be back. It's good to see you, tan and beautiful as ever."

"I know, Dee. I've been waiting for this. Everyone at the shack is stoked to have you moving in. C'mon, let's head back."

My suitcase is lazily tossed into the large backseat, and we settle ourselves inside, waiting no more than a minute before our lips find each other in the front seat of the jalopy. The salt still present on his skin brings me back to the start of this romance. Air pulls away to gift me a flower lei and a large can of coconut water.

"Thought you'd be thirsty after the flight."

"I thought you would pick me up on the scooter," I tease.

"Nah, that scooter stays in South Kona. Now we got the Subaru."

"Ha! You've upgraded."

"I guess you could say that, but this car will be yours so you can cruise and do all your island adventures."

Did you hear that, folks?

The jalopy is mine.

He turns toward me before putting the car in drive and runs his hand down my cheek.

"You are even more beautiful than I remember, Dee."

The jalopy rattles, breaking our enchantment, and lurches forward, taking us back to the shack.

***

We arrive at the base of the steep and bumpy driveway leading to the Dirty Shack's property. The car slips on the rocks and mud, having a hard time making it up the hill. Rain pours down, pounding on the roof of the vehicle and soaking the ground around us. I haven't been in Hawaii during a rainy season, so this is all new to me.

"It's been raining like this every night. You ready to run?"

"Wow, it's really coming down." I peek out my window. "Let's do it."

We exit the car, grab our items, and run like lunatics up the hill, trying our best not to slide into the mud pools. I sprint up the concrete steps and into the familiar shack I've daydreamed about a million times before. Something about it is different, though, very different.

"Something looks different about the shack."

Air laughs, shaking his head.

"It's because I cleaned the floor before you came."

"Ha, no way! How long did that take?"

"Like an hour. Hey, you hungry?"

My face says it all.

"Okay, I'll heat you up something."

He paces back in forth in the kitchen, preparing my plate.

"So, Dee, did you bring it?"

"Bring what?"

"Oh, c'mon. Don't tell me you forgot. It was part of our agreement."

"Oh *shit*. I actually forgot it." My face erupts into a guilty smile.

"What! What will we do now without the hot sauce?"

"I dunno!"

"Here. Check this out."

Air walks over to the dry food shelf and pulls a huge bottle of Cholula from behind a stack of cans.

"I got us covered."

He plates my dish—topping it with cilantro and of course the hot sauce—purple sweet potatoes cooked in coconut oil and coriander, basmati rice, and a side serving of avocado sprinkled with salt and pepper.

The best midnight snack.

Ever.

I scarf down my food, rinse off in the bathroom, and float up to the pagoda.

Our home.

***

"I just remembered how good I felt being around you. I haven't connected with a girl like this in a long time, since my illness. I knew you were the real deal when you spoke about Ayurveda. It took me so long because I was nervous of getting hurt after you left. This island can be quite transient. I see a lot of people come and go, and I never had the desire to get involved on a romantic level for fear they would leave. But you—I couldn't resist you, Dee. I'm happy you're here. I've been telling everyone about you."

He wraps his arms around me as I place my back against his chest. I look around to the rose petals and flowers lining the room in celebration of my arrival. The familiar Christmas lights overhead set the ambiance while stormy clouds surround us, rain now battering against the pagoda's roof.

"I won't lie. I certainly didn't think I would miss you as much as I did. Our story is so beautiful; I mean, we only spent four days together getting to know each other. Can you imagine that? People would think we're crazy, right?"

"If they think we are crazy, it's because they haven't experienced anything like this before."

His arms wrap tighter around me. I can feel the vibration of his words, the joy in them, and the gratitude he has for our relationship. He embodies all the sweetness in the world. I fall asleep once again listening to his heartbeat and breath, but this time my attention focuses more on the loud sounds of the falling rain and whipping wind just outside these makeshift, illusionary walls.

Tonight is a new moon.

A new beginning.

***

His pagoda becomes our pagoda. His car becomes our car. His Hawaiian lifestyle becomes our Hawaiian lifestyle.

Day after day we awake in our full-size bed, slightly damp from all the rain, to the sounds of the boisterous roosters and flamboyant birds. We greet each other with a kiss and a question: "Did you dream last night? If so, of what?" Then we take to the main shack, sip our lemon water, and roll out our yoga mats to begin our practice. Air's commitment to yoga inspires me to get on my mat daily.

Our unique life together is one to be noticed. We went through an adjustment phase upon my return, but we have since moved past that and have a steady routine in place. Air works at a local eatery called Loko Wraps where he prepares tacos and burritos alongside his good friend and creative boss Mike. This further explains his obsession with the hot sauce. I don't blame the kid.

I recently scored a job down the street at a local cafe that serves gelato. I can't get enough of serving dessert. There are no gummy bears at this place, though. I saw the shop, with its clever name, one day while cruising into town with a roommate. We passed it quickly at first, and I was holding my breath until I couldn't take it anymore.

"Hey, can you turn around, like now? I want to stop at Gypsea Gelato and ask if they're hiring."

It is a local mom-and-pop shop run by husband and wife Tim and Sandra, who just so happen to have a passion for the art of crafting gelato. They moved to Hawaii after years of working on fishing boats to bring their vision into fruition, creating their gelato flavors from the local produce of our abundant land like macadamia nut, purple sweet potatoes, passion fruit and Kona coffee, just to name a few. They've been open for about a year and have been running the shop themselves ever since, working six days a week.

Turns out they weren't hiring.

Not until they met me.

My charming good looks and ample experience with treats such as this may have just gotten me a golden ticket inside the door. Not to mention, I'm Italian. Who doesn't want an Italian girl serving their gelato?

I work five nights a week, flaunting my skills, happy to be in a sweet shop again. I can't help but laugh at the fact that I've only worked three jobs up until this point in my life: serving homemade ice cream, serving homemade Italian ices, and serving homemade gelato.

The scooper just keeps following me around.

***

I take a stand, drink in hand, feeling like an island queen on my birthday. Seated at the round table are the loyal and charming faces of my roommates. We have all the island archetypes: the Surfer, the Artist, the Wise Mother, the Healer, the Lone Wolf, and me, the (wannabe) Vagabond. Together we exist in harmony, creating a small tribe of mainland misfits, six people who just happened to stumble across a dirty little shack on a rustic little farm. This is absolutely nothing out of the ordinary for South Kona. I adore these people for all they bring to the table, and I am not just referring to our weekly potlucks but to their contrasting and unique personalities.

Meet Janet, the girl of the water and stars. You can catch her waking up at dawn each morning, waxing her board and heading out for the waves. She tends to the garden and tends to be the one in the house with the largest assortment of herbs and spices. Meet Rissy, a sixteen-year-old-going-on-wise woman. Her floor is always decorated in paints, crayons, canvases, and dried flowers. I go to her for all my issues when I need to hear her wholesome advice, which is typically her saying, "Girl, calm down and go paint something, and bring me a cup of tea."

Meet Lundy, mother to Rissy and a woman of knowledge, well-studied in her craft of bodywork. Just glancing upon her collection of essential oils is life-changing, let alone receiving a massage from her. She once massaged my shoulder for ten minutes, completely relieving my carpal tunnel pain. Meet Emily, the heartbeat of the house. She provides a special touch to her relationships, making all those around her feel cherished and seen. Our random talks bring up revelations about my naivety as she presents much-needed insights to a curious woman like me.

Meet the Lone Wolf, the main chef in the kitchen, the yogi, and the musician: my handsome man. And you already know me: the (wannabe) Vagabond. I'm a woman who yearns for travel, exploration, and culture, life on the road, excursions, and expeditions. I don't know exactly what that looks like, but I'll get there someday. Right now, I have a birthday to attend to.

Everyone directs their attention to me as I make my speech.

"I look around me and see the faces of people who I'm blessed to know. All of you have changed the way I see the world. The enjoyment and laughter is nonstop. I've never experienced a community like this before, and I am truly thankful. This island has gifted me with so much. As the depths in my relationships continue to grow, so do my ambitions. On this evening, as I turn twenty-two, I ask you all to do one thing: look deep down within your hearts and take notice of what your soul calls out to more than anything. What do you long for? What do you crave?"

I watch them close their eyes, breathing deeply and looking within.

"I, as a woman who desires to travel, long to know and be known, to better understand the world we live in and to experience cultures—as many as I can. You all know I have a strong passion to travel this world, just to see what I can see. That is my one wish in this lifetime. I wish to voyage, to travel, to discover who I am and who we are."

I pause.

Young and proud.

"Cheers everyone. Thank you all for being here, and for being a part of my story."

I hold up my glass.

"And thank you to Air who prepared this amazing meal. Cheers!"

My eyes meet Lundy's from across the table.

"Cheers, Deanna; look at you! Here's to turning twenty-two. Gosh, you are *so* young still, like a little bean. You have much growing and learning to do my sweet girl, but it's safe to say we certainly love having you here with us. Oh! I remember the day Air told us you were coming back. I won't lie, I was honestly surprised to hear he has a girlfriend. You should've seen him preparing the place before you came, in a bath towel nonetheless!" she laughs with loving flare and holds up her wine glass.

"Cheers to this beautiful woman on the celebration of her birthday."

"Cheers!" we exclaim in unison.

"And cheers to chocolate and ice cream and all the things this sweet girl loves!"

A toast.

We raise our glasses, sealing Lundy's words, and dig into the colorful food upon our plates: a garden salad with fresh beets and turnips, a coconut curry topped with cilantro, and a delicious serving of tomatoes, avocado, balsamic, and basil. When I'm presented with my cake, the candles flicker and remind me of visions yet to come, potentials yet to be accessed. I close my eyes and begin to cast my spell. My friends sing and clap. I inhale my vision, getting ready to release it.

"Spirit, I want to travel the world so bad. Please, take me to Asia."

The candles blow out, along with my vision.

They applaud and dig in. I can't help but be in my own world, stepping back from the conversation. I notice the silent prayer still emanates inside of me. It makes me feel rather curious, as I've recently arrived in Hawaii and now I'm already longing to take off elsewhere. I sense the calling, though. It's strong, like a magnetic pull or itchy feet. I've been feeling it for some time. My vision to travel doesn't end on this island but extends to the ancient cities of Southeast Asia.

My attention wavers, thrashing me out of my vision, taking me back to the table and to my friends. Janet is speaking to me, asking about our plans.

"So, you two are heading out for your road trip tomorrow?"

"Yeah, we'll cruise out of here after breakfast."

"Nice. You'll have fun. Wish I could go with you."

***

We awake early. I pack my bag; he packs the Subaru.

The car descends the bumpy driveway, up the long and winding road of Nāpōʻopoʻo, through Kailua-Kona, past Waikaloa village, and into the quaint town of Hawi in North Kohala. One road, leading us north. We stop to grab tea and sandwiches at the Kohala Coffee Mill as Air plans our trip ahead.

"So, tonight we'll camp in Pololu Valley. Have you been there before?"

"Nope."

"What? Girl, you've been on this island how long? You'll dig it for sure. After that we'll drive past Waimea and stop at the lookout of Waipio Valley. We can camp somewhere in Hilo tomorrow night."

I sip my tea and nod my head.

"I've been to Hilo before."

"Sweet, we'll get ramen bowls and attend an open mic night. The music scene is fresh there."

"How about the night market?"

"I'm getting there, I'm getting there. We'll arrive in Pahoa with perfect timing to attend the market. Maybe we can stay over at Dina's place. Shoot her a message now."

"How about food?"

He shakes off the question.

"Girl, are you worried about going hungry?"

An hour later, we arrive at the Pololu Valley lookout—grand, mystical, and mysterious. Placing ourselves on the edge of the lookout, the mighty valley quivers with life force beneath us. Created by a series of volcanic eruptions, massive landslides, tsunamis, and wind erosion, Pololu has endured one too many challenges—challenges which created its character. It's a place the Hawaiians revered as sacred for its abundant freshwater supply and nutrient-dense soil, which they used to grow taro in. A place of refuge. A place of solitude. A place of wonderment.

Its rounded peaks dip and dive off into the distance, decorated by pristine foliage, asking us to enter at our own will. I watch at the shoreline bordering the valley, noting their darkened hue as the wind creates choppy waves, making you think twice before entering.

We hike down, cross over the black sand beach, and set up camp deep in the valley. Surrounded by tall dunes and ironwood trees, we nestle in and build a fire to cook rice, veggies, and of course, the traditional cup of tea. Our evening is one of gentle silence, listening to the waves continuously lap over each other. We feel no need for conversation, only the desire to cherish the deep forest and hollering winds.

We take to our tent, laying together side by side, cozy and warm as the wind flickers outside. My eyes rest heavy. Air nods off to sleep. I notice a random spotlight shining down, entering through my eyelids. Quickly they fly open, alarmed.

What is it?

I roll over and exit the tent, cautious not to wake him.

Crawling onto the soft terrain, I'm absolutely stunned to see what I see.

The only light that comes from the midnight sky.

"Woah."

There she is in all her glory, hovering courageously overhead in her rightful place. She is humble yet proud, loyal to her schedule yet not committed to her appearance as she wavers in and out of sight from the clouds blocking her ethereal light. She was peeking through the tent, saying hello to me, asking me to sit with her.

I take a seat among the foliage and bask in the moon, absorbing her light as one would the rays of the sun. She fills me with an inner illuminance, leaving me feeling whole just like her. I close my eyes, begin to meditate and practice the tools that I've been learning these past months at my meditation school. I ground myself, rooting into the terrain below, releasing any swellings of distraction.

Bringing my focus behind my eyes, I'm able to see my inner vision. I'm delighted by the colors arising from my imagination alone, one by one, revealing themselves to me like a fountain of eternity. Fixated by what I'm seeing, I allow the colors to do as they please, now taking the form of an image. First the image appears as a circle, a bright yellow one where other figures begin to take place all around it.

I simply do nothing but allow it to appear, watching it as I would watch a film. The bright circle expands, appearing in the center of a large rectangle. On either side of the border are two tall grey pillars standing in a body of water. It's an image of the moon above the ocean, depicting a vision very similar to my actual surroundings, but it represents the Moon tarot card, the same one I pulled during my reading with Eileen.

Then the imagine flips upside down—illusion.

The moon is on the bottom—deception.

With the next gust of wind, I hear her voice taking hold of me and freezing my vision.

"There's something he's not telling you."

I gasp, my breathing stopping in its tracks.

"Star-crossed lovers."

My eyes fling wide open.

I immediately stand up and shake the image, the words, and the fears from my mind, but they remain inside of me as if they are part of my breath.

I cannot exhale them.

They are within me.

Air.

I wait for my heart race to settle before I climb back into the tent and zip the flap shut.

I lay awake on my back, staring at the blurred image of the moon through the nylon tent wall.

It's an illusion.

***

We park our Subaru along the edge of the damp jungle and follow the groups of people up ahead. Stepping under the roof of the open-aired space, we squeeze our way through the crowds, take a seat at a picnic table, and watch the live performers set the tone. Their large drums beat while onlookers of all ages dance in unison to the vibrations, allowing their loose hanging garb to flow with them. The night sky is penetrated by the low-hanging lights which provide the perfect ambiance for the market.

"You want Thai food?"

"Sure."

"Okay, I'll go grab it. Stay here."

Air lifts himself from the table and ventures off. I disregard his orders and do the same, venturing deeper into the marketplace. I happen upon vendors selling elaborate jewelry, costumes, candles, and herbs. I smile intently and raise my eyebrows as they stare straight into my soul. I pass them all by until I stumble upon a table whose vendor does not care to notice me. Her goods catch my eye.

Behind the table the lone woman sits, her hair styled in two large buns. She has a tattoo of a sacred geometry pattern on her shoulder and her left eyebrow is pierced. She doesn't attempt to lure me in. Instead, she stays put in her seat, convinced her items will do the trick, and they do. I approach her meager table and settle my attention on them. They twinkle and shine, winking at me, withstanding my gaze as I observe their different shapes, textures, and colors. My attention keeps returning to a small opaque stone that sits still, awaiting my touch.

I take it in my hands, and for the first time the lady speaks. Her words are precise, sharp, and to the point.

"Rainbow moonstone."

I don't answer back, but inspect its fine details, noticing the faint rainbow inside of it.

"Good for the frequent traveler—protection. Exposing the subconscious patterns. Promotes psychic energy. Brings about one's intuition and the ability to trust it. Fifteen dollars."

I match her bold way of speaking and hand over my loose cash.

"Done."

Walking back to the table, I see Air sitting with two steaming bowls of red curry and jasmine rice. His head turns back and forth in search of me. Slipping the moonstone into my pocket, I advance toward him with a subtle smile for my admiration of him yet a heavy heart from the intuition that asks me to acknowledge the truth.

STAR-CROSSED LOVERS

———

As the moon spends a few days during each cycle in a state of wholeness, fullness, and transparency, so too does she spend the same amount of time in a complete state of darkness. This is the time where she hides away from the world, keeping her secrets to herself, not willing to show her mystery. This is the duality of the moon. As humans, we live within the same duality, going back and forth from light to dark. There are times in our lives when we live in moments of full vulnerability and honesty, allowing the world to see us in humble totality. There are also times when we resort back to our deeper selves, hoping the darkness will aid in hiding us from the world.

I'm learning daily of this and just beginning to understand why dichotomies are truly necessary for balance in one's life. It's simple enough. Without the darkness, can we even have the light? The moon, through her high state, teaches us to hold on one minute and let go the next, waxing and waning. Through her phases, she teaches us that life is a constant state of change, one we cannot control. Through her black emptiness and her bright fullness, she teaches us that we all have aspects of the light and dark.

I grip the moonstone in my right hand, feeling its edges dig into my palm. Taking deep breaths, I attempt to relax my fluttering heart and all of its anxieties. I've made a promise to myself, and tonight is the night I must honor it. Tonight I will bring the awareness of the full moon to the hidden darkness of the new moon. I will ask him what he is not telling me. I need to be strong and trust my intuition, which is a force both unseen and unjustified. How foolish should it be if the cards, my visions, and my intuition have been wrong all this time?

I think of the potential scenario and my heart palpitates again.

I need to remember.

I need to stay true to myself.

What the cards read and what I saw in my meditations will guide the way.

I hear the scooter pull up to the side of the shack. It hums for a moment before he turns the engine off. Distant chatter inside the house goes off. I know he is making a cup of tea to bring up here.

I breathe deep, then deeper, then deepest, filling myself to the brim.

His steps reach the wooden ladder and he climbs up. I sit tall on the bed, cursing my frantic heart. His eyes meet mine and he smiles, cup of tea in his hands. I watch him get settled, emptying his pack and changing his clothes. He turns on his jazzy music and takes a seat on the bed right alongside me. Throwing his head back, he exhales loudly then stretches his arm out to me.

I don't take it.

He looks up and taps me with his hand.

"Dee."

I remain silent, my face flushed.

"Dee, what's up?"

How will I be able to mutter the words I know I need to ask?

I need to summon all the inner strength I have.

"Dee?"

"I have a question for you."

My voice is stern. It catches his attention, sending a bolt of anxious electricity from my heart to his.

He knows.

He sits up straight, alert, and faces me.

"Yeah?"

My gaze hesitates to meet his.

I am ashamed, guilty even, for having to do this, but who would I be if I didn't?

"Did you?"

He laughs.

"What?"

I say it again.

"Did you?"

"Dee, what are you talking about?"

"Please, just answer my question. Did you have sex with her?"

His face flushes, draining of all his beautiful color, turning both as pale as the full moon and dark as the new moon.

"Dee..."

I don't reply.

"I'm sorry."

"Yes or no. Did you?"

The entire blackness of the night drops down with all of its weight and lands right inside my chest, holding my breath hostage and stealing the Air from my body.

***

We both exit the pagoda, me first and him following.

The tarot cards had, in fact, been correct.

My intuition was accurate.

My deepest fear has come true.

I walk toward the main shack, heart ailing, ready to collapse, and in need of comfort. Air follows behind me, trying to explain himself, I suppose. I don't want him to catch up. I have nothing to say to him. Yet the exact moment both of our footsteps arrive at the entry way to the Dirty Shack, our roommate Lundy steps outside with a blissful smile upon her face.

She sees us as she always does: two youths with stars in their eyes. She positions her body perfectly so that she stands directly in between the two of us, as if planned. Unaware as to what has just transpired, she places her strong arms around our shoulders and points our attention toward the pitch-black night sky.

I allow her to act out her joyous charades, looking up into the starry sky only to be greeted by the absence of the moon. Lundy shifts her weight and gets her voice real low, as low as she possibly can before it becomes a whisper.

"Just look at those stars, my children," she sighs. "Take a moment and look at their beauty."

Her strong grip tenses around our shoulders. The stars glimmer and glisten above our minuscule heads, responding to her admiration. I'm in a state of complete heartache, not wanting to do anything other than dwell over it, but my body is somehow softening, and I do as she says. I stop focusing on the absence of the moon and I look up to the stars, blinking from above, praying that someone will notice them.

She speaks again, this time with an even more bone-chilling lowness.

"Tonight, those stars..." she exhales deeply. "Tonight, those stars shine for you, my loves."

There it is.

Star-crossed lovers.

I don't know who she was, but I know there was a "she."

A "she" other than me.

And he confirmed it.

The breath inside my body exits. What once inflated me now leaves me deflated and void of air.

Tonight would be the last night the stars would shine for us.

The illusion of love is no match for the storm of infidelity.

***

The first lesson of Air is the lesson of duality. Every truth is an illusion, and every illusion is a truth. The lesson of duality asks us to consider all things, seen and unseen, as a potential reality. Air is nowhere, yet everywhere, at any given moment. It takes us through a journey of lightness and darkness, good and bad, beautiful and horrendous, so we can experience the contrasts of each. Without these contrasting aspects, how would we be able to tell the two apart? Both sides—both moons, new and full—need to be acknowledged in the Fool's journey if they are to ever advance.

The second lesson of Air is the lesson of change. The harder we grip onto thin air, the more our tendons ache and ask us to relax, if just for a moment, and allow the air to be as it will: free-floating and without solid form. Air holds an illusionary quality which asks us to fall in love with things as they are, yet to also allow permission for constant change. That's because there is not just one way of existing. Air itself is a free-flowing state of evolution, inspiring us, like the moon, to enter our next phase until a full circle is completed yet again.

The third lesson of Air is the lesson of perception. How we perceive our world is reflected by how the world greets us. The truths that exist through our perceptions only come from the meaning and importance we give them. Though again, like air, perceptions and beliefs are not concepts meant to be fixated in place. Air is a gentle reminder that formulating truths and perceptions, no matter what they are and how they are obtained, is like building a castle on a wall of thin air, a pagoda-shaped castle with a full moon in the center.

***

I slump down on Rissy's floor, my head hitting the wall and knees pulled close into my body.

"Did you just find out?"

"Yeah, just now."

"Do you know who she was?

"Says her name was Trisha. But who knows if he's lying about that?"

"Damn girl. I'm sorry that happened. It's good to know the truth, though. So, if you're planning to leave, where will you go?" Rissy asks me over the music, drawing in her journal.

I stand up slowly, body aching. I'm still in a state of disbelief; the magnitude of the scenario hasn't fully hit me yet, and I know it. It's a defense mechanism saving me from the pain yet to come. I walk over to a world map plastered on her wall.

"I'm going here."

She looks up, half-distracted.

"Bali?"

"No."

My finger drops away, marking the name of the city.

"Vientiane."

"Oh. I don't know where that is."

"Me neither. But I'm going."

"You're not nervous?"

"Of course I am, but how could I ignore the signs? It's all meant to be, Rissy. Look, I need to earn my stripes on the road. This is exactly what I've been yearning for. I'm ready to be altered by the Vagabond life."

WATER

THE GREAT EXPLORER

——

On the lofty day of February 26, 1992, two crows, black as night, sit high atop a thin electrical wire hovering across the street from a hospital in the suburbs of Paris.

"Where've you flown to today, ol' Ruth?" coos the darker crow.

"You know, Harry, the usual. Over the sixth arrondissement. Good God, I was dropping shits all over the place. Nearly got a buzz from the cigarette fumes. If the French smoked any more, their lungs would be as dark as our coat. "

"Agh! Agh!" Harry and Ruth hoot and holler from atop the cable, clearly enjoying their winter migration from London a little too much.

An elderly man who sits on a rusted bench just below looks up from reading *Le Parisien*. His grey hair is nicely kept in a small beret and a cigarette rests between his crusted lips.

"Putain de corbeaux. Ta gueule," the elderly man huffs and grunts, smoke exiting his mouth through his coffee-stained teeth.

The crows find the anger of this man rather hilarious, so they continue on and on, cackling like only crows know how to cackle.

"Hey Harry, did you hear that? I speak French now. He's telling you to shut your trap. Agh! Agh! You're sitting right above his head. Go on now. Give him one, aye? Agh! Agh!"

Most folks are unaware, but when a crow shrieks at its loudest, that is laughter breaking through, for crows see things that humans do not—humorous things.

Easily distracted from a commotion across the street, Harry ignores Ruth's comment and redirects the conversation.

"Ruth, you silly little flapper! Quit your squawking and check that out over yonder."

From atop the voltage cable the two crows, black as night, give three little hops, scooting to their left. Soaring high above all landscapes, one can only imagine all the spectacular sights a crow sees in just twenty-four hours, *especially* in Paris. Yet these two crows now glare at something rather unusual.

"My God, Harry! It's a peculiar thing, isn't it?"

"I do say so, Ruth. I do say so. It looks like he hatched just moments ago from his little egg."

"Do you think that's the mother, Harry?"

Both birds redirect their laser beam focus from the face of the bundled baby to the young woman who carries him.

"It ought to be, Ruth. You see how she is holding that thing? Must be her first."

The two crows stay perched on the wire with their beaks shut tight, only for a brief moment, as they watch the newly blessed mother, father, and their newborn son interact. They have just exited the hospital and are now bound to bring the baby boy home.

During her first moments of interacting with her newborn son, as he sits nestled in the warmth of her arms, the subconscious intuition within this mother already senses the tenacious character of the baby she has just birthed. A mother knows her child best, even within seconds of their initial encounter, and this deep intuition inside of her will soon prove to be precisely and incredibly accurate.

"He's a wild one Ruth," Harry claims. "I can see it in his eyes. You see that too?"

Just as Ruth begins to answer with another one of her smart-ass comments, a strong gust of wind blows from behind them. Seemingly appearing out of nowhere, perched on a wooden pole that connects to their cable, stands a bristling and shining raven. The raven's feathers hold a hue blacker than the non-color black itself, outshining the dull black of the two crows. The raven balances in an upright posture, showcasing his pride with an unmatchable glaring gaze.

The raven is silent.

"You've got to be kidding me. Ravens in Paris? What's next, Harry? Flamingos? Have I lost my feathers?"

"Ruth, shut your quacker. Can't you see, you idiot? This is a raven from the land of spirits." Harry whistles in a low shriek out of the side of his beak as he takes notice of the deep blue aura emanating from the raven's presence.

"Oh. *Shit*." Ruth's breathing stops right in her tracks, as she fears she may have already disrespected the spirit bird.

All birds can recognize with ease when a spirit bird is near, and a spirit bird often emerges for good reason. The two crows roll their gaze toward the raven, offering their "utmost" respect knowing that ravens are highly respected birds of the sky, but a raven from the land of spirits is a different story, for they arrive with a purpose.

They arrive with messages.

The spirit raven speaks.

"I was summoned," his great voice echoes.

Harry and Ruth shift back and forth on their perch, becoming overwhelmingly uncomfortable.

"I was summoned," the spirit raven bellows once more.

At this, Harry grows astonishingly annoyed, forgetting that this raven is spirited.

"Well, it was not I, raven. You see, we did not summon you. We only sit perched upon this cable observing the cinematic French life below us. There was no call to you through the beaks of us!" he screeches loudly, making his point.

The same elderly man from below hears the loud squawks of all three birds once again. Having reached his patience with their listlessness, he flings his newspaper into the air with force screaming, "*Quel bordel!*" before shuffling away from his once-peaceful bench.

This catches the attention of Ruth and Harry, who can't help but break their beaks in laugher, cackling like children at play.

"Agh! Agh!"

The spirit raven stays unruffled by the stupidity he witnesses before him and halts their guffaws with a question.

"Where is the baby?"

Harry and Ruth gape at each other, their heads tilted in a state of stupor.

"The baby? The baby!" Harry screeches.

"The baby, baby," Ruth follows.

"That's why he's here!" they gasp in unison.

"Down that way, uh...royal raven spirit, sir," Harry answers the question with a jester-like bow and hop.

The spirit raven fixes its gaze on the young mother holding the baby boy in her arms, bundled in a blue blanket.

"There he is," the spirit raven says to himself. "This is the child I have been summoned to protect."

"Good luck with that!" Harry bellows, losing all manner of respect yet again. "You see those eyes, don't you? Like I said, good luck. Spirit raven or not, that baby is a tsunami!"

The spirit raven looks back at the crows, slightly perturbed by their stupidity yet in awe of his next assignment: to protect and watch over this baby boy throughout the duration of his entire human life. He stands taller than before and begins his speech.

"There is no human too wild for the raven spirit. There is no human too berserk for the raven spirit. When the protection of the raven spirit is summoned for a human, it symbolizes a great life is to be lived. This baby boy, as you see him now, looks vulnerable and helpless, even strange perhaps, but one day he is to travel across all the oceans. He is to pace himself through the trails of many mountains. He is to become a Great Explorer. Not all humans are born with such grand destinies. He comes from the brightest star of them all."

The spirit raven waits before speaking again, choosing his next words carefully.

"This young one has a celestial mission, one I will make sure he follows. Through his life experiences and travels to come, he will be presented with obstacles and opportunities to sharpen his many skills, for he is to become a conduit between the natural world and the spirited world. It may take him many years and many hard lessons to learn, but he will build a bridge from the soil to the stars. He will quench the thirst of this lovely Earth."

The spirit raven, upon completing these words, spreads his mighty wings, flaps them four times, and flies with great speed straight toward the baby boy. He leaves behind even more stupefied crows who are baffled by what just took place, questioning if it ever really happened or if they inhaled too much cigarette smoke. Scanning everywhere for any sign of the spirit raven, they see nothing but a faint aura of indigo blue surrounding the baby boy. An indigo blue that had not been there just moments before.

The new mother enters the vehicle with her son on her lap, and off they ride into the distance.

***

The young mother watches as her sweet baby boy turns into a young child who arrives home from school one after-noon and longs to set his kindergarten on fire. The spirit raven is indeed present for this, emboldening him to feel all his emotions. Years pass in front of her eyes and she now watches, without concern, as this same child interacts with the world around him, not harshly but peculiarly. The spirit raven indeed observes this too, encouraging him to ask all his questions.

She notes without effort that her firstborn son is quite the genius, quick to his own perceptions and opinions about the environment around him. The spirit raven has already been quite aware of the boy's genius, which is the main reason why he had been summoned years ago. She also sees he is a passionate fighter, displaying tantrums of rage mostly rooted in his sensitivity and compassion for the world. The spirit raven eggs him on during these bouts of passion, influencing him to always follow his curiosity and trust his intuition.

This now-experienced mother observes openly the way her son grows into a juvenile, thus developing further his patterns, friends, lifestyle, and personality. The spirit raven plays a big role in the development of all this, pushing him to extremes. She has come to deeply adore her firstborn child, though physical distance is to be put between them because this now young adult has decided to take his very first trip from the meager suburbs of Paris to the bustling city of Buenos Aires.

The spirit raven will never be separated from the child.

The spirit raven will fly with him.

Faced with the concerns most mothers would feel at this decision, her worries are present, yet few and far between. Since her intuition has been accurate all along, she also trusts her son's intuition will light his path, but it's the spirit raven who really is the one to magically gift her a peace of mind by visiting her, not once but twice, in her dreams.

During the first night that spirit raven enters her dream, he does not say anything to her. He just glares, allowing the mother to absorb his golden presence. On the second night, the spirit raven appears again, more golden than ever, and says five words which puts the mother's heart fully at ease.

"Your son is with me."

On the third night, the spirit raven has already flown off with her son, and the mother enters a restful and deep sleep. Only after having observed the past seventeen years of her child's life, she knows deep down that her son must see the world at large.

The spirit raven has known from way before the boy's birth that he, at once, must see the world at large.

That he is to be a Great Explorer.

***

As the story is told, his aunt offered to purchase him a ticket to anywhere in the world, so long as the Great Explorer has the unyielding tenacity to take the trip, which he very much does.

So, he takes it.

He arrives in Buenos Aires and speaks very few words of Spanish.

He feels fear and excitement intertwined together, but upon arrival he steps out of the bustling airport and lays his maturing eyes on his very first Latin American sight: a beaten-up yellow taxi parked on the curb. Leaning against the bumper is a large-framed man smoking a cigarette.

Given his French nature, the Great Explorer enjoys seeing this man smoking on the job. He walks straight up to the guy and flashes him a smile. The man takes one last suck on his smoke, flicks his cigarette to the curb, opens the door to his taxi, and turns his head to exhales the smoke. The Great Explorer bows his head humbly and enters the beat-up vehicle without saying a word.

Off they drive into the city of Buenos Aires.

In a matter of moments this man-turning-boy picks up the Spanish language and picks up friends from here, there, and everywhere. He picks up routes and maps, yerba mate, and ceviche. He gets picked up while hitchhiking, he picks up cocaine from the locals, and picks up his fork to feed his curious and starving mouth. The Great Explorer picks up his charisma, new perceptions, and his life experiences.

The spirit raven applauds it all.

At the end of his six-month trip he returns to his unwavering mother, completely wavered and more tenacious than ever. His first trip through Latin America acts like a drug, birthing in him the desire to hit the road once more.

His mother is slightly surprised that her son wants to continue his travels.

The spirit raven is not surprised at all.

The Great Explorer carries on in the way he unhesitatingly does, filling the years of his early twenties with as many human experiences as ever. He fuels his newfound addiction of traveling with different places, locations, cities, and people. He rides the trains throughout Europe and swims his way to shore during a rough tide in Greece. He goes to the outback of Australia to live in a dysfunctional van while in a dysfunctional relationship. He bids his time in the United States while indifferently visiting more states than the average American resident.

The spirit raven sits back and watches the show, having to step in only a handful of times.

The Great Explorer suddenly finds himself in South East Asia, both physically and spiritually speaking. The spirit raven has decided the time has come for the young man to take an even bigger step—a step to further develop the plan he established before his own birth. The spirit raven encourages the Great Explorer in many mystical and esoteric ways as he divinely provokes the occurrence of certain people, scenarios, and conversations throughout this journey.

The Great Explorer continues to be altered.

The Great Explorer is constantly put to the test.

The spirit raven eases back and watches as he pushes on and on throughout his travels in South East Asia. Many questions come to the surface, about which the Great Explorer is forced to contemplate. His style of traveling has become so refined it is effortless, like a flowing river.

He's always in flow.

One day, the Great Explorer decides to purchase a motorcycle from a mechanic in Hanoi, Vietnam. He slaps down 4,635,000 Vietnamese dong on the table and takes the keys from the counter.[2] Walking toward his new bike, he runs his calloused hands across its dried leather seat. He ties down his hefty bag to the rack with bungee cords and takes out a folded map from his back pocket to contemplate his upcoming travels. He's already traveled through Indonesia, Malaysia, and now Vietnam.

His eyes trace the map, noting his next obvious destination: Laos.

"Nadine."

He smiles at the bike.

"Allez."[3]

He crumples the map and shoves it into his back pocket, ties a turquoise fabric around his head, and plops on his helmet.

Straddling Nadine, he starts her with ease. Together they drive off, exiting the shop and entering the busy streets of Hanoi.

The spirit raven follows them over the tall Laotian mountains, through the deep jungle, and straight into the capital city of Vientiane.

---

2 Vietnamese currency

3 Let's Go

ONCE UPON
A MOTORBIKE

——

The station around me hums. So many people are here, shuffling to-and-fro, selling salted nuts, fanning themselves with newspaper. Everyone seems to be in their own world, distracted by the sticky heat that makes itself known.

I am one of them.

I stand from my seat in the hectic train lobby, stretching and recalibrating. Outside the station darkness prevails, while inside bright fluorescent lights puppeteer my circadian rhythm. I lift my backpack, fasten it onto my shoulders and hips, and begin to walk to the train boarding area. With each step I take, my pack sways to the left, right, left right, making me feel like a horse with a saddle. I look down at the small-printed ticket in my hand. Written in blue ink are the numbers I need to make sense of if I ever want to leave this station.

"Train: 208B

Seat: 1055 A

Boarding Time: 21:00"

I double-check my phone for the current time and venture beyond the lobby doors into a very large chamber of trains. Coming and going, arriving and leaving. People pour out of them and walk toward me. People walk away from me and pour into them. A man in uniform blows his whistle, half-ass directing the traffic while assisting passengers in finding their trains.

I enter the noisy cellar-like structure and pace past each of the trains, looking for the golden number 208B.

I see 208A and 208C.

"Typical," I think.

I walk back to the man in uniform and show him my ticket. He looks at me.

"Typical," he thinks as he rolls his eyes right after landing them on my backpack.

Together we walk no more than ten strides. He stops and points me to 208B, exactly where I had been standing before. I bow my head and offer a flustered smile. He walks away without saying anything, blowing his whistle in the distance as I enter the train.

I find my seat without a problem. It's a bed, as this is an overnight train. I imagine the ride to be like the movies, falling asleep on a lullaby platform while rocking gracefully back and forth, passing through thousands and thousands of kilometers of history, cities, and terrain, all while being served tea and biscuits. I'll certainly have ample time for random journaling sessions where I write down all my secret thoughts and revelations of being a Vagabond, only to arrive to the magical destination after a full night's rest.

Oh, the foolish wonderment.

Instead, I'm greeted with frigid temperatures thanks to the nonstop air conditioning blasting stale air onto our backs.

A hard-surfaced platform serves as a bed with its one thin white sheet. The food being served is not warm herbal tea and biscuits, but grilled chicken on a stick which resembles intestines or some other delicacy. I sit on the bed and put my backpack underneath it, pulling out my journal, earphones, and a pen. The lights inside the train match those of the fluorescent ones in the station, once again playing jokes on my circadian rhythm and my wonderful fantasy of overnight train rides.

The train begins, lugging slowly out of the Hua Lamphong Bangkok Train Station.

There are only nine hours left of rest before I reach my magical destination: Vientiane.

If I'm even pronouncing it right...

***

"We arrive!" The thin curtain to my bed flies opens, making my very first sight of the day the face of a curious young Thai woman. She wears a white uniform and holds a steaming pot in her hands.

"Coffee for you?"

"No, no. No, thank you." I fan my hand and send her on to the bed across from mine.

"We arrive."

Locating my glasses, I sit up and take a peek out the window to my right. The sun is just beginning to show its face through pastel shades of pink and coral.

My heart flutters.

I'm *really* doing it. I've waited long and hard for this adventurous moment, and though I carry little bags of grief inside of me, curiosity is clearly the master to this movie.

The train begins to slow.

I reorganize my backpack and pull out my passport, ready to apply for a Lao visa on arrival.

***

"How much is it to rent?"

"Oh. That one is seventy-three thousand kip per day—good bike."[4]

The store owner nods his head ferociously, bobbling it up and down.

I grab the handlebars to the lime green bicycle and roll it forward.

"I'll rent it for three days."

"Okay, okay, no problem. Passport, please."

Just as I reach for my passport tucked inside my fanny pack, I hear the noise of rippling engines approaching our street. They are loud, clearly, as they grab the attention of both me and the shop attendant. The noise grows, approaching from afar and closing in on us. Our transaction is on complete pause until we see the source of this noise.

In the flash of a heartbeat, with the speed of a humming-bird, three motorcycles rip past us and continue down the road. I blink a few times, processing what I've just seen. A sensation of frustration arises within me as I grip firmly onto the frilly white handles of the bicycle.

"How embarrassing," I think. "This green piece of shit versus those badass motors." I should hide my face in the long line of tourists that come here daily to live out the same

---

4   Laotian Currency

experiences. I dismiss the deep shame those motorcycles catalyzed in me, along with the adventure I long to have.

"You still want to rent green bike?"

The shop attendant, most likely feeling the same insecurity from those motorbikes, latches on nervously to my expression.

I rip the burning desire from my chest as I hand him my passport.

The streets are no match for me—or rather, I'm no match for the streets. Loads of people and a plethora of vehicles are on the roads, crisscrossing and intersecting constantly. I'm unstable on my green bike, nervous and awkward. I hit the curb many times, swiveling out of control while passing through large groups of people, nearly getting run over. I hide my accumulating shame and push forward.

And I make it.

To the National History Museum of Laos.

I park my bike and enter inside the large white building. Walking slowly through the long halls and spacious rooms, I see artifacts, pots, costumes, chairs, and instruments. To be honest, I hadn't known Laos was a country until just a few months prior when I located Vientiane on a map.

Do you *really* think I would know anything about its history?

Because let's be honest, I'm an American.

I'm in complete shock as I enter a room that greets me with hundreds of circular objects hanging from the ceiling. They are spray painted in a gold-tone and they represent bombs. The room is filled wall-to-wall with photographs and inscriptions. The photos are aged, ones of military aircrafts, and leaders. I step in front of a photo showing an outline of Laos. It's scattered with green dots, showcasing all the regions where bomb clusters were dropped from the US Air Force. The entire map is filled with green dots, from eastern to central Laos, signifying the horror of the situation.

I read the description below it, exposing myself the truth that I was unaware of.

"Throughout the course of ten years, from the mid-1960s to mid-1970s, the USA released more than two million tons of bombs across the entire county of Laos. This makes Laos the most bombed country in the world, in relation to its size and population. During that time, many of the bombs landed but did not detonate, leaving around seventy-five million bombs which are still ticking time machines. These undetonated bombs are mostly a risk for farmers in the countryside and children, as they have had brutal tragedies in the years since and up until present day."

My heart seizes.

How could I have not been aware of this?

I didn't think traveling would be this painful, but this just points a finger to my sheltered ignorance.

The truth hurts, doesn't it?

I look to the faces of the local Laotian people, thinking about the pain and suffering my country has caused them in the past. I realize something quickly. This isn't going to be the first truth to startle and hurt me. There are going to be many of them coming on at full speed, showing me just where my upbringing and sheltered life faltered dearly. I'll be picking up the clues of history along the way, but I have a lot of catching up to do. How embarrassing. But let me be humiliated, for humiliation and exposure are the only ways to erase ignorance.

***

I sip on a small mug of black tea that embodies an aggressive flavor. A man comes with a plate of food and places it directly in front of me on the picnic table: two rubbery eggs, a piece of toast with berry marmalade, and a banana, along with this small mug of aggressive black tea. Wonderful combination. I pick up my fork to dig in. When someone brings you free breakfast, don't question it. Eat it.

My bag is packed and ready for movement, with my yoga mat strapped to the outside and all. It sits inside the lobby of the hostel I've been staying at since my arrival in Vientiane. The hostel has been jam-packed with sweaty travelers coming and going, in need of a cold bed, a warm shower, and free breakfast. I had hopes of making connections, but that's hard to do with a shut mouth. Shyness consumes me, causing me explore the city on my own and go to bed early. I've missed my all chances as today I fare onward on a large touristic bus to another large touristic city.

This isn't really the adventure I've had in mind with comfortable hostels, roomy buses, and a lack of relationships. I'm a novice and I know it. That's the worst part. Traveling is a skill I haven't yet acquired, but hey, we must start somewhere and earn our stripes along the way.

But I'm ready to kick it up a notch.

My week here has been as good as these cold, rubbery eggs.

And that's giving credit.

I'm somewhat embarrassed to be an American, realizing how little I know about the matters of life outside of the red, white, and blue and how uptight I truly am. Tension rides right alongside the oxygen in my arteries. I've been watching how the others act—the Germans, the Swiss, the French, the Australians. They're always at ease, smoking cigarettes and creating conversation full of laughter. I notice how they sit, relax, and enjoy. Something, I'm also not skilled in. I've never been taught how to *relax*.

How to enjoy.

I split my rubbery egg in half, beating myself up for these arising insecurities while two blonde women sit across the table from me. They look like they've known each other their entire lives. One of them articulates a story in accented English, probably German, speaking louder than necessary and drawing my nervous attention toward her.

"Oh yeah, we just came from the north, it was incredible. We were lucky to get the girls through the mountains."

She grabs for her small camera.

"I have photos of where we slept a few nights ago. It was on a boat. I fell asleep right near the edge."

She pauses, concentrating on her camera.

"Here it is. You see that? I could've fallen right over the edge in the middle of the night."

The other blonde takes the camera in her possession, observes the photo, then hands it back. My heart races, suddenly longing to be a part of this conversation.

"Here's a photo of the guys swimming. You should've seen them in the morning! When I woke up, they were already diving in to go for a swim. I thought them crazy but joined minutes later."

On and on she babbles, almost speaking just to make me jealous.

"How were you allowed to sleep on the boat?" the other blonde finally speaks up.

"The guys asked the fisherman to let us sleep there, and he said yes. It was by far the coolest place we've camped so far."

"So where will you go next?"

"We're heading south and taking the girls down there to camp."

"How many of you are there?"

"Originally there was just me and Vaidas. We met in Vietnam and made our way to Laos together. Then we met another guy and asked him to join us. We each have our own bike, and Sophie will come now as well. She'll be riding with me."

The woman who shares all these lovely details is smiling from ear to ear, as if she has fallen in love with the life she lives. I can tell she is young and joyous, yet fiercely brave. From what I understand, she's been traveling on a motorbike for the past few months. I'm both inspired and insecure, for I long so badly to be like her.

She's a firecracker.

I want to ask her how she can do it and tell her I'm dying to do the same.

I'm just too damn possessed by doubt.

I look down at the limp egg on my plate and then glance at my pathetic backpack propped up against the nearby wall.

"We keep finding ourselves in these amazing situations. It's so great to travel on motorbikes because we can go anywhere we want with them. There's nothing stopping us."

As I bring the marmalade toast to my mouth, I discover an inner challenge. The longing inside of me has swelled up so ferociously I'm afraid I will drown in it if it goes unseen. I slide forward on the bench and sit up tall, placing my elbows in the table. I must speak. I must ask her. I can't let this pass me by. On and on she chants, making me work for an entry.

I'm thirsty.

And the only thing to quench my thirst is an adventure.

Fuck it, I want in.

"Did you say you're riding on motorbikes?"

My voice comes out stern, as if I am testing her, not believing in her excitement.

She brings her yapping to a halt and turns toward me, looking down at my rubbery egg then into my eyes.

"Yeah, we are. They're old girls. A little beat up, but that doesn't stop a good ride. Honda Win remakes. We each bought them in Vietnam." Her smile surprises me.

What do I ask now?

Don't be American, please don't be so American.

"Oh, wow. Are you actually *allowed* to do that? I mean, travel on them and camp everywhere?"

She looks at me as if I've come from another planet—a planet called America.

"Uh, yeah, of course. You just have to be smart about it."

I almost don't believe her.

"So, where are the bikes?"

Without hesitating, she looks blatantly past my right shoulder, holds out her arm as far as she can stretch it, extends her pointer finger like a magic wand, and says, "They're over there."

I turn around in a cinematic slowness, following the guidance of her outstretched hand, and what I see next is just too perfect for American eyes like mine. About thirty feet out, on the other side of the road stand two men, one short and one tall. They hold on to the edges of a bright blue tarp and, in unison, they flip it off the items underneath it.

That's when I recognize them—the three motorbikes.

Characterized hunks of metal flash a steel smile at me, tempting me like a seductress once again. They sit perched atop their kickstands, awaiting to be saddled and taken for a ride.

"Poison Ivy, Hera, and Nadine. Those are the girls."

Her voice calls me back to reality.

"We may actually have an extra seat, though you'd be crazy to join."

What did she just say?

Taking her words as mockery, I drop my eyes down to my cold eggs, questioning why she would tease me like that.

"It's true."

A shadow is cast over me.

"Jojo is right. We do have another seat, if you want to join."

I don't see the source behind the voice before I smell the smoke of his cigarette. I turn around to see the tall man looking straight at me.

I hesitate to respond, his certainty intimidating me.

He forces out between puffs on his cigarette.

"Show me the size of your bag."

I take a stand as if I am on autopilot, no longer interested in my free breakfast, and I walk over to my backpack, scoop it up, and hand it directly over to him.

He takes it.

"Seriously. That's it?"

"Yeah. That's everything."

He tosses it up and down.

"It's light."

Without reluctance he walks across the street and straps my bag onto the rack of the middle bike. My eyes don't leave him as he takes full control of all the contents I currently own.

He walks back over, cigarette still bummed between his lips and phone in his hand.

"It fits great. We're leaving in ten minutes. Be ready."

"Wait, what?"

"I guess you're joining us," Jojo teases while standing and walking away from the table.

I have no choice now. I haven't given them an answer. An answer was given to me.

Have I gone mad?

I question myself as a hand is placed on my shoulder. It's the same tall man.

"My name is Vaidas, by the way. I'll take your bag on my bike, but you won't be riding with me. You'll be riding with that guy." He nods his head once, motioning at a figure walking toward us from across the street. It's obvious that he is the only other guy in the group.

"Good luck pronouncing his name." With that Vaidas walks away, leaving me in a dazzled state.

I stand up from the table, preparing to introduce myself to the young man approaching, the person who I will be trusting with my life before even meeting him. I take notice of his quirky stance as he walks forward with his hands on his hips, not so much in a flamboyant way but in an "I just got shit done" kind of way.

He is wearing a vibrant turquoise-stitched band around his golden, shoulder-length hair, keeping it out of his eyes. His jawline is prominent, and he hosts a quiet smirk, gentle and knowing, growing with excitement as his cheeks redden. His skin is kissed slightly by the sun, matching the few highlights in his hair. The shirt he wears on his lean frame matches the color of his headband but displays an African design of shapes in turquoise and white.

He walks straight up to me, bold and brash, until his eyes are all but a few inches from mine.

"So, you're joining us, I hear?"

"I guess so..."

"Ah, very nice. I am happy to see another joining. My name is…"

His name is thicker than the accent itself. I hear it clearly, but I don't know what letter it could even possibly start with. It's like a tongue twister, sudoku puzzle, and foreign language all in one.

"What?" I ask, puzzled.

"It's…"

"I'm sorry, I don't understand you." Now my cheeks redden.

"Just call me…"

He now throws out a shortened version of this indecipherable noise and I *still* don't understand him, but act as if I do.

"Oh, okay. It's nice to meet you."

I bow my head and smile, laughing the matter away.

Well at least I *was* warned.

"I told you!" Vaidas calls out from not so far away.

***

The deed is done.

All three bikes now roar with life, creating the same thundering rumble I heard at the bicycle shop just a few days earlier. The only difference is that I now sit among them, ready to fly off as fast as that hummingbird. We're a group of five, me being the fifth addition to this band of Vagabonds.

I take up the backseat with my helmet on loosely. My driver, whose name has left me at a loss of words, throttles the engine.

He turns over his right shoulder.

"You ready?"

"Yes!"

As we're about to ride off, I look up and see Jojo stopping alongside us.

"Wait a second," she calls out to me over the hum of the engines. "We don't even know your name. We don't even know if you're," she extends the last word, riding off and screaming it out loud for all the street to hear, *"craaaaazy."*

Me...?

...Crazy?

Nah.

My body is rapidly jerked back as the bike lurches forward, following right behind Jojo's voice.

I surrender to all those American anxieties and allow myself to forgo the doubts. I've received my initiation and I know it. I am one of them now, an adventurer. I know from the deepest place in my heart that this group has already accepted me, and they will now begin to show me the skills of navigation.

"Hold on," he calls out to me.

I do as he says and slither my nervous arms around his foreign waist, having no choice to but trust him in this voyage.

My thirst is about to be quenched by Water.

VAGA-BONDING

———

It's my very first night with this group of Vagabonds and here I am standing like a virginal child, watching the sloppiness of humans on their best-worst behavior. I don't second-guess my decision to join this group of European bikers until I see the haven of ground that is to become our deluxe night of sleep. The group explores this determined "campsite" by parking their bikes and wandering off into the fields. Jojo is already splashing in a muddy bank while Vaidas and Water are packing their bamboo bong with local herb and Sophie finds the nearest tree to slump against like a worn-out log.

I stand still, negligent to my purpose, and ponder what sorcerer has cast this spell. Whoever it was, and for whatever reason, they have performed skillfully. Five curious cats from five different countries all brought together in a melting pot of hundred-dollar motorbikes, mud-crusted tarps, and a bamboo bong which keeps breaking—just these ingredients alone are enough to entertain the gods, and I believe I can hear them applauding from all the way up there.

"Hey, new girl. Come with me to get some beer."

Vaidas starts Hera and slides his body up the seat. I oblige and let the gods watch the scene change.

Into the ramshackle town we drive, in search of none other than beer—well, beer and whisky. Laotian people are a funny breed. Their diet alone consists of bland soup and tormenting whiskey sold in used plastic bottles. To travel Laos is to adopt this diet. Another ingredient for success, or failure, depending how you look at it. Vaidas parks Hera alongside a dilapidated hut where a robust woman comes out to scowl at us.

I watch from the bike as he plays his role perfectly: a tall, exaggerative expat communicating his needs without hesitation. His clumsy attempt to speak with the shop owner only further validates her lack of interest in him. A conclusion is finally surfacing; I can sense it. Vaidas is now being handed what looks like twenty beer cans and two plastic bottles which house a clear liquid. I see him pick up a small tomato and three eggs from a wicker basket. He observes them and adds them to the purchase, for good measure I assume. Bowing his head, he waves goodbye to the woman, carrying a knapsack of delight.

"See, we made a friend."

I look behind him to see the woman closing her front doors and shutting off all the lights.

"Doesn't really look like it."

"She sold us the rest of her rice whiskey. That certainly sounds like a friend to me."

He starts up Hera with a harsh kick and our miniature voyage continues, but dusk has fallen fast on our way back to camp, leaving Vaidas lost, stressed, and longing for a beer.

"I thought it was this way, but that just seems to be just a pile of weeds."

We continue onward for another thirty minutes, Vaidas navigating and me having nothing to add except for silence.

His grunts communicate his dissatisfaction with the scenario and his shoulders tense up. I breathe heavy and remain hidden behind him, hoping he will forget that I'm here.

He hasn't forgotten.

He stops the bike and turns it off. It is here where we sit for a startling two minutes before Vaidas vocalizes himself.

"Get off."

The godly trumpets in the sky are now playing as they watch the scene below: little virginal me obeying the man's orders. I keep my breathing low and slide off Hera. Here is certainly where I will meet my match. He'll leave me out here. I know it. I'll have nothing—no phone, no wallet, no wits. What a great plan on his end. It's so brilliant, I actually should applaud him for it. Soon I will perish all while pondering if the sorcerer and the gods are truly laughing now.

He looks up at me, and I see the frustration through his thick-rimmed glasses. His grip tenses around the handlebars, causing his knuckles to flex in a frightening manner.

Shit.

Yup, I'm done.

We do not break eye contact. I refuse to go down in fear. My face holds strong. I clench my teeth.

Did I ever think I was tough?

Well, now I need to be.

He takes in one deep inhale, letting it slowly penetrate and flare his nostrils.

"Deanna, we have an issue." His voice is still stern. My eyes still match his. "I've dropped some beer in the distance, and you must be the one to gather them. Take my flashlight and locate them. No beer shall get left behind."

Are you kidding me?

That's what this is about?

The goddamn beer?

I've clearly underestimated my match.

God-damnit.

I snatch the headlamp from his outstretched hand and stumble into the grassy field. How did he even notice? I turn over my shoulder and he's still sitting there, back toward me, perplexed and riddled though it seems. As I go on my mighty search for these fallen soldiers, I realize that I need to check myself, possibly toughen up a little bit.

Or loosen up.

That's it. I need to loosen up. I'm an uptight girl from America who hasn't experienced much of anything other than sales racks at TJ Maxx and occasional campfires with Jersey bros. Alongside this group is exactly where I need to be. They aren't just wild, rambunctious, and ridiculous.

They're free.

I walk back with two cans in my hand, no more, no less.

Another one of God's perfect plans.

I pop the tops off and push one of the bottles into Vaidas's chest.

"Aren't we lucky."

"Only two, huh?"

"Only two." I confirm.

"Hmm. We shall enjoy. Cheers to being lost."

I turn off my headlamp and together we sit side by side, in total darkness, drinking our lukewarm Beerlao.[5]

"So, Vaidas. Tell me. How do you pronounce his name?"

"Who?"

"The French guy. How the hell do you say his name?"

---

5   The beer of choice in Laos

"*Ha,*" he lets out a casual laugh and chokes down his beer, "I don't know. If you say it wrong, he'll get pissed. Mark my words, no one in the group has yet to master it. Good luck, kid."

I laugh.

It's funny, right?

"Well, what should I call him?"

"Oh, right. You're riding with him. That must be freaking awkward. Just make something up or avoid it altogether. That's what I do."

"He'll notice eventually, no?"

Vaidas nods his head in realization, crushing his can and plopping it into his sack.

"Yeah. But I'm sure it's not the first time. He's a wild one. C'mon, let's get back to them. I want to finish these beers."

With a new wave of encouragement, we locate the correct trail. Vaidas sounds his horn the entire way, playing an unplanned game of Marco Polo. The others await us—us and our beers. Just wait until they see our considered abundance.

We pull up next to the two other bikes.

Ah, home at last.

"So, what did you guys bring back for dinner?" Jojo walks toward us.

I turn silently and look at Vaidas, smirk on my face.

"Oh shit, my bad. I totally forgot about dinner."

"Vaidas, we asked you to pick up some ingredients! What the hell did you get? You guys were gone for a long time."

"Well," Vaidas pats his knapsack proudly. "We got lost, and we got beer. Oh, and whiskey. We got whiskey."

A male voice cheers from the behind the fire pit.

"Wait," I chime in, "what about the tomato and the eggs?"

"Oh. They fell out along with the beers back there."

I smack my palm to my head.

"Sophie, he only brought back beers," Jojo calls from behind her, blinding us with her headlamp.

"Oh, great. Well at least I have those leftover buns and a jar of peanut butter."

"Dammit, Vaidas. You're fired!"

We gather around the camp, Jojo stoking the flames, Sophie cutting the buns in half, Vaidas looking at a map while drinking his beer, and Water staring hypnotized into the flames. I take a seat among my newly adopted family. They pay me no attention as I pay them all of mine. They're in their element, like children who have finally gotten away from their parents' harsh demands.

We've been on the road just one day and I'm wholesomely coming to enjoy them.

But really, do I have a choice?

"So," Water's accent breaks the silence between me and him. "What brings you to Asia? What is it you are running from?"

I note the way he pronounces Asia: "Az-ee-ya." I have two choices: ask him to repeat the statement so I can hear his French accent once more and humor myself, or be a champ and answer his question.

Hmm, I'll be polite—for now.

"What brings me to Asia? All I can say is that I had a vision of traveling here and felt the need to fulfill it. You ask if I'm running from something, but I would like to say I'm running toward something."

He looks at me now; his eyes squint and lips smirk.

"Hmm, as it's said, you will find peace of mind when you realize the thing you are running from is the very same thing you are running toward. So, what is it that you are running toward?"

Shit. I'm speaking with a philosopher now. I'm cornered. My hands go up. He already knows.

I have nothing to lose by being honest.

"Myself."

"Then we are the same. I knew I liked you when you decided to join us."

"So, you've come here in hopes of running from yourself as well?"

He takes a swig of the beer, his eyes back on the fire. There is certainly a confidence in his arrogance—the short sentences in which he speaks, his blunt tone, and his opinionated perceptions. I like it.

"Baahh. *Oui.* I not only run from myself. I also run from the government. It's shit, in France and all over the world. The way of life in Paris, with all the people who are already dead, doing what they are told. I travel to find a different way—a good way of life. The simple life, with very little problems, nice people, pretty girls, good friends. That is the good way of life."

I listen a little too attentively to what he lays out before me. Shouldn't I have known? I mean, look at his eyes. They tell it all as they mirror the flames in front of him. I see a deep-seated longing in him which has yet to be fulfilled. This longing seems familiar, but maybe I am just looking into the sunken eyes of another weary traveler, one who has taken off from his family to satiate such empty spaces inside of himself. A deep hole exists within the hearts of wanderers and it just keeps getting bigger and bigger with every new place they stumble or any new person they encounter.

Maybe we're not so different after all.

"Even though I've traveled many, many places, Asia has always been my top destination. I have waited a long time before I come here." He pauses. "I know this trip will bring me something I search for, or at least I hope for something like this."

He sips the last of his beer and leans forward into the fire. Without using a stick, he grabs impeccably at a toasting bun with his bare hands, slinging both away from the hot coals at the same time. The bun comes flying toward us and lands on the grass.

Smearing peanut butter across the bun, he rips it in half and, without taking his eyes off the flames, hands a piece to me. "I always am traveling alone. I like it this way, but I'm happy to be a part of this group and happy to have you riding with me. This is the road to the good life. Salud," he holds up the bread and finishes it in one bite.

"Salud."

***

We exit the never-ending marketplace and make our way toward the bikes. I lag behind the group as they huddle in deep discussion over our next plans, Jojo and Vaidas bickering as usual. I've decided to avoid ever getting involved, as they have it all under control. I'm just along for the ride. I'll leave my lack of experience on the outskirts, thank you. I'm aware of my role among this crowd as the follower.

We've been on the move ever since leaving Vientiane, not staying more than a single night in any location. Four days of consecutive camping, and it's been the longest I've gone without taking a shower or checking my phone. I don't miss such distractions, as the rivers and waterfalls we've been stumbling across suffice my soul.

In fact, to put it honestly I'm high on life. The sensations which arise when I get on the bike are altered from anything I've experienced before. The past doesn't matter, and the future does not yet exist, so who the hell cares? Only in the present can bliss be so certain. Is this what all motorcyclists feel? If so, it's *always* worth the risk. To die in bliss is to live a Fool's dream.

It must be the wind, or maybe the constant murmur of the motor. Perhaps it's the immense exposure to the sun, or the cascading mountains that enclose us. Whatever it is, I'm a fan, a follower, and a disciple. Each time we stop for breaks, I long for the moment when the engines throttle once more. I don't drive the bike, for it's not my place, but sitting passenger is enough to enlighten me in this once-in-a-lifetime adventure.

How about the man who I ride with, my chauffeur turning partner in crime?

I still cannot say his name, though I must be honest: I haven't given it much of a try. I've taken Vaidas's advice and each time I address him I simply just say, "Hey." If he's noticed, he hasn't said anything, so I will keep this method until then.

Throughout these past four days I've come to better understand his role in this group: sometimes the follower, sometimes the leader, though typically he is game for whatever, especially the hilarious ideas and antics of Vaidas. Water is an interesting one. Having traveled, it seems, the most out of all of us, he still greets each and every place we visit with wonderment in his eyes, attempting to fill the deep hole of longing I noticed in him on our first night together.

His obsession with food is something to note, as we have this something in common. Our conversations are few and far between, but not because we have nothing to talk about.

A lot of time is just spent behind him on the bike. When we do speak, I like what I hear. His concepts are intense, viewpoints are well thought out, and his sentences are blunt and to the point. We have a similar sense of humor, which has been bridging the gap between us. I look up to him and his bizarre stories of vagabonding the world, which explains the reason behind his ridiculous behavior, like the other day when he climbed on top of a tall rail and jumped, legs out, onto his idling bike.

I held my breath while the others had laughed.

"Does this guy ever get injured?" I thought.

I finally catch up with the group and stop in front of Nadine, who is different from the other bikes. Her body is painted forest green and adorned with a sporty red and blue streak down the side, giving her a vintage appeal. Her mechanics are quirky and difficult, mimicking her operator, Water, as she resists shifting gears when asked. She has character and spirit—good ol' Nadine.

Water hands me his only helmet, as he's been doing ever since we set off together.

"Thank you." I smile, and I place it over my head.

"Welcome." His accent is thick.

He watches as I pull my hair back and fasten the buckle under my chin. I look up, our eyes automatically meeting. His focus quickly shifts with a jolt, turning his head and attending to the bike. I blush and turn toward Vaidas.

"Alright, team. We're in for another adventure today," he speaks. "I'm checking out the map here. If we continue at a good pace this afternoon, we'll arrive to Si Phan Don by daybreak. Let's plan to spend a few nights there. I know of many hostels in this area, so I'm sure we could find a cheap one."

"You know where to go?" Jojo chimes in.

"Of course, we just follow the Mekong River." He lights up a cigarette. "When in Lao, always follow the Mekong River."

"How long will it take until we get there? Should we bring food or at least snacks for the way?"

We all turn toward the Swedish voice of Sophie. She has a careful way about her, that one, and may be more anxious than I am. Either way, she is good to have in the group because Sophie is the only one who remembers we are mortal humans in need of food and rest. She is thoughtful and sincere, handing off her snacks to us at every stop.

"Nah. There will be plenty of beer stops along the way. Trust me," Vaidas answers, a puff of smoke leaving his mouth. "Besides, didn't you all eat breakfast in the market?"

We hesitate on answering the question until I start giggling.

"We filled up on those fried dough balls again."

The four of us break out laughing.

"Again? All of you?" Vaidas asks, looking at each face.

"Yeah. He ate like fifteen fried balls," Jojo says, pointing toward Water who pats his enlarged abdomen.

"You're all ridiculous. Okay, enough of this. Let's get going, we're wasting precious beer time!"

Vaidas already has his engine started and rides off, leaving the rest of us full of shitty fried dough and laughter.

***

Today's journey is hot and long. With my legs straddled over the bike, I can feel the sun directly above my head, but the wind dissipates any buildup of heat. Since I'm more comfortable with riding passenger, I keep my hands on my knees and away from Water's waist, though I caught myself earlier rubbing my palm across his back in an adoring caress.

It happened naturally, and when I realized I pulled back, hoping he hadn't noticed. I'm still questioning how this act slipped past my awareness and occurred so effortlessly.

Must be the sun.

We arrive close to our destination around mid-afternoon. The damp air greets us with a fresh and mysterious aura. Vaidas pulls over alongside the road and motions for us to join him. The three bikes line up so we can hear his wise words.

"Let's look for a hostel along this road, that way we can put our bags down and let the bikes rest."

We each take a sip of water and follow his lead once more.

As our bikes weave through a small and quiet dirt road, we slowly roll up to a colorful wooden building. Sitting near the edge of the road, a sign painted in English boasts of cheap and clean rooms for rent. We park the girls, slide off the hot leather seats, and make our way indoors.

"Only two rooms available. Two people per room. No more," the receptionist details.

We take a moment to discuss our next option but as we turn around, Vaidas is unraveling his camouflage hammock and explaining to the man in exaggerated motions that he would like to sleep in it tonight and let us four have the rooms.

The receptionist stares at Vaidas.

"Okay, okay. You may have the rooms. You must set up sleeping hammock outside, though. Enough of this."

He waves his hand to end the confusion, leaving Vaidas in a state of victory.

We follow the receptionist as he grabs two old keys hanging on a wooden wall beside him and walks through a back door. Out back we are greeted by another run-down wooden building and a literal pig pen. I look down, blinking six times before adjusting to the commotion. Over thirty piglets are running around with two huge mamas lying flat in the midday heat among a plethora of chickens and ducks.

"Vaidas, you're sleeping with the pigs tonight," Jojo calls out, making us laugh.

"I would prefer goats, but I'll accept the pigs."

"Do not touch!" the receptionist yells and motions toward the mothers. "Very dangerous."

Jojo and Sophie carry their bags into one room, leaving me with no choice but to claim the same room as Water. Vaidas takes his unraveled hammock and strings it up on the porch beams in between the two rooms. He kicks off his smelly boots and tests it out, eventually falling asleep.

His loud snoring inspires us all to do the same, retreating to our rooms for an afternoon siesta from the hot sun.

***

I awake to the group chatting outside my door. I must be the last one up.

Quietly joining, I take a seat alongside Water on the porch steps. He puffs on a cigarette that Vaidas hands him. Despite his crazy outbursts and bad habits, I'm starting to feel a familiarity to his presence, as he also has a calming and soothing aspect about him. I'm just realizing now that my unpredicted little action earlier today of rubbing my hand across his back had come out of pure care, for he both intrigues me and concerns me with his intellectual flare-ups.

"So, what do you think?" Water now turns his attention to me behind the smoke of his cigarette.

"About what? This piglet pen?"

"No," he exhales a cloud, "I'm talking about the bikes. What do you think about traveling on them?"

"I actually never thought I would do something like this... ever. I feel so happy to be with you all."

He takes another puff, and without looking me in the eye, he proposes a question which startles my heart.

"So, you want me to teach you to drive, Nadine?"

In seconds, visions of every potentially dangerous outcome run through me like a flash flood. What would my parents say? What if I crashed? I've never driven a bike before, and I have no idea what to do! Would my feet even touch the ground? My mind chatters away, pulling me farther and farther from his question.

"Deanna?"

I jolt and come to my senses, swallowing the mind chatter.

"I would love nothing more."

"Right now? I believe we are about to leave for the waterfall hike," he puffs again.

Oh shit.

I act calm, but inside I am a hurricane.

"Sure."

He can sense it.

"Don't worry, I'll teach you. I'm a very good driver. It was my job in Paris." He puts out his cigarette and stands.

Jojo approaches us with a knapsack.

"Hey guys! Sophie isn't joining us; it'll be just us four. You ready to go?"

Water looks at me and smirks slyly, answering for the both of us.

"Yeah, we are."

TEST DRIVE, FIRST KISS, AND THE SECOND BURN

———

It begins to drizzle slightly. That doesn't matter.

I've never driven a motorcycle before. That doesn't matter.

My feet hardly touch the ground. That certainly doesn't matter.

I'm handed the helmet, as usual, but this time we reverse our roles. Now I turn over my shoulder to look at him.

"What're you doing? You're not wearing shoes, or a shirt. You're crazy for trusting me this much."

He laughs without care, buzzed from today's sun.

"Well, you're crazy for trusting me. Let's go. Allez!"

As he reaches over my right shoulder to start the engine, he begins to explain how to work the clutch and shift gears. I have little understanding of what I'm being told and hearing the words through his thick French accent makes it even more challenging. All I can do at this point is trust him and, of course, myself. He places his damp hand over mine and grips the clutch. After he lifts the kickstand, I go ahead and put the bike into first gear.

Slowly letting off the clutch, I wobble forward.

"Allez, allez."

Without understanding the words, I understand what they mean. I let go of my tight grip around the clutch, allowing the bike to roll forward even more.

"Allez, Deanna. Let's go. It's easier when you speed up; give her a throttle."

My left hand releases synergistically from the clutch as I give a little play to the throttle. The bike responds by urging forward with more power than before.

"Allez! As you speed up, shift the gear!" Water is screaming now, leaning over my right shoulder, his bare skin touching mine. His ease with this whole situation gives me the confidence I need, so I keep my hand on the throttle and shift the bike into its next gear.

In a matter of seconds, I'm doing it. The bike speeds up and cruises at a steady pace. The straight road in front of me is completely empty except for our friends up ahead. I shift gears again, picking up more speed than ever. Water is watching what I'm doing meticulously, grabbing onto my waist now with his left arm.

I feel we are the only two people alive in this moment. The sky casts a grey hue above us, where twinkling drops of rainfall. My attention is hyper-focused, my adrenaline rushing and my confidence rising, along with a daring smirk across my face. I'm only wearing shorts and sandals. It's not proper riding gear, I know, but I'm young and this is fun.

The growing mist kisses my face and illuminates the road ahead. This whole moment is magical. I feel Water come closer to me, his arm growing tighter around my waist as he speaks into my right ear.

"That-a-girl."

His warm body presses up against mine in the same way mine presses up against his whenever he drives.

The engine is picking up speed, going above fifty miles per hour.

"Not bad at all!"

I'm smiling and squinting my eyes, a luminescent and worthwhile grin on my face as I come up close behind the others. When they see me they cheer, glancing over their shoulders.

It's simply a moment of bliss.

The others start to slow down for our destination and my bike begins wobbling a little bit, as I am having a hard time coming down from such a high speed. Water lurches from behind me to grab the handles and bring us off to the side. The bike slips a little, but we're safe, pulling into a dirt lot alongside the others.

"Your feet don't even touch the ground," Vaidas points out.

"Yeah, but she did good. Now she will be my chauffeur."

"I wouldn't recommend that. You know how tricky your gearbox is."

Water grins at me.

"I told you I would be a good teacher."

"Hey guys!" We hear Jojo's voice trailing from afar. "Let's hike up before the sun sets!"

I follow their lead, gripping my thin sandals onto the muddy and slippery trail, adrenaline still racing through me, until we arrive at the top of the upward climb. Ecstatic and out of breath, we plop our bags down while Vaidas pulls a water bottle from his bag. He shakes it and smiles.

"Time for some LaoLao."

"Is that...?"

"It is—rice whiskey."

He takes a swig, swallowing hard, and hands the bottle over to me. I place my nose over the opening and smell the ferocious fumes.

"Ugh."

"Just try it. When in Laos we drink LaoLao, or Beerlao. Either will suffice."

I bring the bottle to my lips and take a small sip. The sharp and penetrating liquid enters my mouth, causing me to gag in a hilarious display. The whiskey has no choice but to flush down my throat, and I am instantly heated from the inside out, becoming one with the LaoLao.

"It's disgusting," I say as I hand the bottle back to him.

"Disgustingly strong. Who else wants a sip?"

We huddle together on the cliffside, sipping the rice whisky and undressing, allowing our heart rates to simmer down. When our gazes finally lift, we are greeted by a fairy-tale-like scene: tide pools. Tons of them. Tiny ones and large ones. A small waterfall above us delicately deposits a well-spring of fluids into the rock-carved pools. The water bubbles up and overflows like a fountain of youth. There is an edge, a very tall one. Off this edge is a great waterfall standing over a hundred feet high. We can see the entire town in the distance, with its soft streetlights twinkling at us through the mist.

The sun lowers off in the distance, blessing the tide pools with rays of golden yellows, periwinkle, and creamy orange. It's by far the most incredible sight I've ever seen. My soul feels kissed, altered, and elated. I'm truly on top of the world.

I follow the lead of the others to the wellspring. They look like children at play, completely naked in this surreal moment. We dip in and out of multiple pools, testing the waters of each and soaking our bodies in the perfect temperature. Our conversations have faded, and we absorb the view around us. I take in my humble surroundings and the faces of the people who sit beside me.

Maybe it's the rice whiskey, or the high from driving Nadine, but something in me clicks, aligns, and surrenders to the realization that I'm home among this tribe. I've come to absolutely adore all of them, individually and collectively. Smiling with one another, sharing jokes and conversations endlessly, these folks have been teaching me how to live the good life—a life of nature and simplicity, friendship and adventure.

We meet along the sharp edge of the tall waterfall, sitting completely naked, side by side, and looking down at the drop off below.

"Okay guys, this is serious. Absolutely *no* joking around while we're sitting here," Vaidas teases.

We laugh, subtly agreeing to both the beauty and danger of friendship.

***

On our way back from the waterfall, I ride backseat with Jojo and Vaidas rides with Water. We're all a little tipsy from the LaoLao and decide it a wonderful idea to race. The bikes begin slowly side by side with the drivers yelling profanities at each other. Jojo picks up speed, pushing her bike Poison Ivy past its limits, while Nadine comes up fast.

"Go, Jojo, go! Don't let the guys beat us."

"I'm trying!"

Just as she picks up a little speed, Nadine appears directly across from our left side and hovers there. The two bikes are matching speeds now. Water turns toward us, his sculpted face and devilish smile glowing through the mist as he screams over the engines.

"Let's join."

He reaches out his right hand.

"You're crazy, no!" Jojo screams back.

But before she notices, my left hand reaches out and grabs onto his. We lock fingers across the small space between us, holding on tight.

"Dee, you're crazy. Don't do that," Jojo yells with a smile.

Nadine picks up speed, encouraging Jojo to concentrate harder, pumping Poison Ivy faster and faster until we make it back to the hostel.

All in one piece.

***

We sit around a large rectangular table to share a great meal with other travelers. I'm eager to take a seat next to Water after our waterfall experience tonight. Any gaps between us have now been bridged; a bond has formed and there is no going back.

"Thanks for letting me drive today."

"Thanks for letting me teach you today."

I smile and notice his usually arrogant smirk has turned into a soft wave upon his face. It invites me to stay a moment longer than normal, seeing the once obvious emptiness in his eyes are now an open heart.

We practically inhale our meal the moment it reaches the table: fried rice, thick noodles coated in spicy sauces, and bowls of steaming soup. The best part of adventurous days is coming back to the food and eating as much as we desire.

With heavy eyelids and full bellies, we all make our way back to our hostel.

Water and I say goodnight to the girls, check on Vaidas asleep in his hammock, and slip into our room. I leave to change and wash up, only to return to Water curled up and potentially asleep. His body lays across the middle, causing me to take the shrinking edge. I turn off the lights and sink under the thin covers.

In the same way I had felt the warmth of his body come closer to me during our bike ride, it now joins my side again. His hand reaches out, taking mine. We lock fingers, bridging together the small space between us, holding on tight for a second time this evening.

I freeze, but the blood inside of me moves faster.

Is this really happening?

Foolish me.

It has been obvious all this time.

I just didn't want to believe it.

He comes closer, resting his head right above my heart, his wavy light brown hair falling upon my chest. I place my hand on his head and run my fingers through his hair, welcoming his gentle embrace by simply staying still.

His lips meet mine just once before he speaks.

"I really like you. I don't know why, but I do."

Still thawing out from my frozen state, I continue to hold his warm body in my arms. Together we fall asleep, side by side, fingers clutched, dreaming the dreams of voyagers and vagabonds alike.

***

With grace, our travels continue.

We take our bikes on roads weaving through lush green mountains. We take our bikes through dusty trails kicking up sand and stones in our faces. We take our bikes to the shorelines of rivers and the edges of trailheads looping through the thick Laotian jungle.

Each day presents challenges, yet each day also presents solutions. We find ways to cook dinner with very few ingredients. We create ways to set up camp for a good night's sleep anywhere and everywhere. We speak with locals even though they can't understand us. We find locations off grid. We make friends everywhere we go, while still enjoying the company of our original group.

Today is a hot and humid day, one where our plans have fallen through, raising tension between the group. We're lost in a small village with darkness quickly closing in on us and nowhere yet to sleep. It's beautiful here in this small fishing town, but given the day's struggles, we all have a hard time appreciating it.

As we weave our bikes through the narrow trails, looking for an exit, the path out in front of us becomes dense with mud. I'm riding on Nadine with Water, as always, and we are leading the group. We trudge on, the muddy road worsening and giving the bike a hard time making it through. Nadine slides back and forth, causing my heart to accelerate.

Water seizes control at the last second each time.

A strong intuition comes to me. It's the strongest I've had in ages and presents itself like an actual voice speaking aloud to me.

"Deanna, get off the bike."

I tap Water on the shoulders.

"Stop the bike here. I'll get off and walk. It'll be easier for you to maneuver through this mud."

He turns to me with an intense certainty.

"Relax, Deanna, I won't let us fall."

I sit quiet until this inner voice comes again.

"Get off the bike now."

Once more I tap upon his shoulder.

"Please, let me down. I want to walk."

This time he completely stops the bike and looks at me.

"You really don't trust my skills? I promise we won't fall, Deanna."

Nadine lugs on. With the weight of me as a passenger and our bags on the rack, she sways unsteadily. The mud doesn't let up. We hear shouts from our friends in the distance.

"Be cautious."

Water is attentive, but the mud is too much, and it consumes us and his promise. I tumble and he tumbles. The bike is on its side with my right leg pressed in between the exhaust pipe and a small wooden fence.

I immediately remove my leg as quick as I can from the scorching heat. But I'm clearly too late. I'm not wearing proper gear, and the searing pipe has left its detailed signature in the form of a second-degree burn on my right calf. It's already blistering, leaving me limping to the other side of the road in a state of shock.

The others approach us.

"What happened?" Vaidas parks his bike immediately and comes to examine my leg.

"I asked him to let me off." I grit my teeth in frustration, my leg starting to throb.

"It's going to be okay. This happens more often than you think. I already have a plan and here's what we're gonna do."

His confidence soothes me only slightly as the pain has no mercy.

I stand, helpless and still, as he takes out his worn plastic water bottle that holds LaoLao inside of it.

"Start drinking." He passes the bottle and its buoyant liquid over to me.

I resist. "I don't know, Vaidas. I don't really want to."

Now he kneels. His eyes meet mine and he begins to educate me in his hilarious way, summoning a voice that communicates his support and humor. I listen as he speaks, but I'm slightly distracted as an entire group of local village children have now encircled us, staring with bright and curious eyes.

"Look around you, Deanna. You have a whole audience here, just for you! Hey, look at the little guy over there."

He lifts his head up toward a naked toddler running around, flashing his butt cheeks our way.

"That little guy came out here just for you. Aren't you lucky?"

I look up to see the little tyke. The scene is hilarious, and the humor does me good in a moment like this.

"Deanna, listen." Vaidas grabs my attention once more. "You're in remote tropical village in Laos and you fell in mud. You will need to clean out this burn or it could get badly infected. I've gotten many burns during my days of riding and I always apply burn cream and clean them out exceptionally well. You'll need to do the same, and I'm sorry to say, but it's going to hurt. But taking a few sips of this guy," he holds up the bottle and shakes it, "will take the edge off."

Before I can count to three, the rim of the bottle presses to my lips. I quiver as the first shot makes its way down my throat, heating me from the inside out. I follow it with a second shot and a third.

Hey, he's right. This stuff ain't so bad after all!

This stuff just happens to make the whole world so easy to forgive!

So easy to forgive—until my eyes meet his.

He is upset. I can see it on his face.

He should be, I think to myself as I look down to see the sangria-colored scar upon my leg.

"Dee, I'm sorry. I was arrogant for not letting you off when you asked," Water speaks aloud with everyone listening.

I hear what he says. Without responding, I lift the crumpled bottle up to the rim of my mouth for a fifth time. After I swallow, I limp behind Vaidas, choosing to ride with him over Water for the first time ever. It'll give him something to think about, and for now I'll enjoy the buzz of pleasure and pain.

***

I ride with Vaidas until we reach a small hostel along the Mekong River. Now completely tipsy, I barge into my room and head straight for the shower, ready to clean off this burn like a champ. I scrub all the little pebbles and dirt off its edges, wash it with soap, and dry it thoroughly. I meet the others in the lobby, and Vaidas pours alcohol over my burn. I don't feel a thing.

We plan to stay three days in this hostel so we can rest and recalibrate, for soon our group will be splitting up. I'll have the time to relax and take the initiative to perform some healing measures on my burn as well as connect once again to my meditation practice, as it's been a while.

I slump in my bed, no longer buzzed but confused. The pain in my leg has faded into a constant and gentle reminder of a time where my intuition spoke loudly yet I did not listen.

Now, when I feel the need to speak to my spirit, it appears there is no voice to be heard.

"What's going on here?" I ask for clarity.

"Should I continue traveling with him?" I ask for guidance.

"Can I trust him?" I ask for truth.

Each question comes back without an answer.

I think about Water and his intensity and flares, but also his heartfelt emotions and softness, which I've seen just as much of. I don't want to be mad at him. I know it wasn't his intention, but I'm certainly frustrated with his arrogant ways. We will be sharing a room again for these next few days and, strangely enough, I appreciate it.

The door opens, and he enters.

Speak of the devil.

"Hello."

He bows his head low and closes the door gracefully.

"Hey."

Sitting on the bed alongside me, he takes my hand in his.

"I know I won't make it any better, but I'm sorry for my arrogance. I should've let you off the first time. If you still want to ride with me, I'll make sure to let you off whenever you don't feel comfortable. I promise."

He bends down and kisses the back of my hand.

"How're you feeling?"

"Better, but still a little shocked. The whiskey is wearing off."

"May I lay down with you?"

I slide over, allowing him space to join. He sails his body next to mine, once again placing his head on my chest, holding my hand firmly. My heart sinks and floats, sinks and floats like a buoy. He's taken me along for a ride—an emotional one, testing my intuition and my ability to surrender to trust.

I pull him closer. I forgive him. Of course, I do.

But do I forgive myself?

Am I going to go on judging myself only for what arises naturally?

I like him.

There, I admit it.

I like him.

Despite his rather uncontrollable, explosive, intense, and frenzied way of being, I like him—a lot.

How could I admire a man this wild?

How could I admire a man this out of control?

But, then again, how could I not?

Only when all waves in my mind come to a complete stop do I feel the cascade of his lips meeting mine in an intimate second encounter. His frame drifts above me as he slides one arm under my back to embrace me further. His eyes meet mine. I see their story clearer now. He is a vessel that is in need of constant fulfillment, movement, and experiences. He doesn't want to be controlled, but he does long to surrender to his own self, and right now he is asking me to surrender to him.

I can't, at least not yet. I see his longing bellow out into a state of wanting, willing, and waiting.

He is wanting me to surrender, willing to make love happen, and waiting for my answer.

Like a large body of water that sits day after day, wanting, willing, and waiting to be entered. Wanting, willing, and waiting to be surrendered to. Wanting, willing, and waited to merge boundaries. His emotions pulsate through me like a flood, drowning me in his passion as he kisses me again and again. His breath rises and falls like the ever-changing tides. I'm just able to stay afloat, keeping my head above the surface.

I'm not yet ready to sink and surrender to Water.

***

Three days pass before we hit the road once more. I flinch when my eyes fall upon Nadine, robust and beautiful as ever, waiting for us to take her across the Mekong River. I've been treading a wave of emotions since parting ways with Vaidas and Sophie.

Now it's just me, Jojo, and Water. We take the bikes across Laos and to a road that crosses over to Vietnam. The route we have chosen to take is sandy and steep, which provokes my newfound anxieties. It isn't until later in the eve that Nadine once again slips to her side and beautifully imitates her driver by offering me a steamy second kiss. Now I have two burns in the exact same spot.

Where is Vaidas with that LaoLao?

BAREFOOT AND BOUNDLESS

I sit with my back against the bed frame, knees bent, and legs curled up close. Cozying up, I reach one hand for my feet as the other dials my father, who exists quite frankly on the other side of the world. The rickety fan makes laps, fanning dry air and dust straight into my face. I hear my father's voice scramble spastically through the phone line.

"Hello. Hello, Dee. Hey, Dee."

"Charles!"

"How's it going? Are you still traveling with that group of Germans?"

"No, not anymore...and Charles, c'mon, they weren't all German!"

Yes.

This is what I call my father: Charles.

A long-standing joke that lives on in legacy.

I look up to see Water pacing the room, looking for the army knife that he loses in nearly every city.

"Only one was from Germany, and the rest were from different parts of Europe—Lithuania, France, Denmark."

"Lithuania? Where the hell is that?" his voice jumps through the phone line, humoring me.

"It's somewhere in Europe. Don't worry about it," I fan away the topic while watching Water unpack his entire bag, distracting me only slightly.

"Okay. Well, are you still traveling together?

"Well, we almost all went different ways. Jojo flew down to New Zealand a week ago to continue her travels, Sophie returned to Denmark, and Vaidas decided to stay in Vietnam. So, it's just me and the French guy now." My grin rises like a crescent moon upon my face as he looks up from his endeavors with a perplexed glare.

"Oh, okay. You guys are getting along good?"

"'Well, we haven't killed each other yet."

"Oh, that's good."

The joke clearly flies over his head.

"So what's his name again?"

My laughter thrashes, illuminating the phone line, Water still staring curiously into my soul.

His name?

Right, right. That thing.

We have spent well over a month together and *still* I cannot pronounce the poor guy's name. Throughout the past few weeks I had given it a go, but very clearly butchered it, embarrassing my own self and pushing any future attempts back down the depths of my throat.

"Well, the thing is, Charles," I keep my eyes unwavering on Water's, "I know it, but I don't know how to pronounce it."

"What the hell do you mean you don't know how to pronounce it, Deanna? You've been traveling with this guy and you can't pronounce his name? What do you call him? Just the 'French Guy'?" His Brooklyn accent extends through the phone.

I nod fervently.

"Yes, actually, that's exactly what I call him!"

"Alright, Deanna. Well, find out his name for me. Anyway, stay safe, please. We miss you over here."

"I miss you too, Charles."

The phone call ends but my smirk remains.

No longer is Water fixated on finding his knife. He stands with his hands on his hips, offended, with a perplexed set of eyes.

"You really don't know how to say my name?" his accent spills out but doesn't showcase his emotion.

I smirk humorously, having nothing to say in return.

"French guy, huh?" he pesters again with more attitude.

"Well, you're French, aren't you?"

"Okay. I see how it is," he dips his head, raises his eyebrow, and opens his mouth in slow response, "Jersey Girl."

My eyebrows fuse, crinkling my smirk into a sour expression of questioning.

Is that supposed to be funny?

After seeing my face change, he bursts out in grand laughter, wearing his victory like a plastic crown.

"You don't like when I do it to you!" he continues, doubled over now.

I brush off his words and walk away, but beyond me he relishes in his own amusement.

"Ahah! She doesn't like it!" He continues on and on.

***

This is how we get along, pressing up against each other in such a way that it surfaces our humorous flaws to purposely speculate them further. Once a weakness is in full sight, he or I grab at it, tossing it to-and-fro like a giant multicolored beach ball, laughing and enjoying the game we've created for ourselves. Don't fret—it's done with pleasure, for our own enjoyment.

It's the way we vibe.

The amiable teasing manifested itself after my second burn, when we decided to lock ourselves into the commitment of traveling together. When we said goodbye to the others, we were left standing and facing each other.

"Now what?" I asked.

"Come with me," he proposed.

The answer was obvious.

If we aren't camping, stringing out our cheap hammocks across palm trees, or being hosted by Buddhist monks in temples, then we stay the night at a cheap hostel. Our typical method is to pay for two beds but utilize only one, so that we can snuggle together like two drifters afloat on a small twin mattress frame. We are content as a pair of love birds who have finally found each other overseas. He is the steersman and I'm the loyal follower. Most of the time I have no clue which city we are headed to or the current city we are in. I just wholeheartedly trust his skills of navigation and comply with foolish glee.

It's symbiotic, for the most part.

When the sun sets over the ever-trailing Mekong River, we walk the darkened streets side by side, me listening and him recounting stories of his times in Cuba, Greece, and Australia. We walk so close together that our shoulders constantly brush up against each other, nearly in competition for the narrow sidewalks. We have a connection which emulates two separate stars of the same constellation. We are conjoined at the hip like mainsail and mast, synergistically moving our boat of love across the changing tides of experience.

He is hilarious, always making me laugh with jerky movements and his hairy French mustache, which I constantly ask him to shave. He refuses to wear shoes, preferring to walk barefoot through the polluted cities and roadsides. A fellow traveler we met in Bangkok finally took notice of the barefoot Frenchman after an hour-long conversation and, in a state of shock, asked, "Dude, what happened to your shoes?"

On occasion he wears a rope around his waist, for a belt is unnecessary and only takes up space. Though the rope is supposed to simulate a belt, it does a poor job of completing the task. Every time he bends over, his crack presents itself to the world, which leaves the locals flinching and me doubled over, grabbing my stomach in laughter. His backpack is ridiculous. It's a French military backpack from the 1970s with leather straps that refuse to break no matter how much he tugs and tugs. Its endless spaciousness gives home to a hammock, a tarp, many articles of clothing, two toiletry bags with kittens on them sewn by his mother, a sleeping bag, a towel, a headlamp, a journal, three books, and a large cigar box filled with gemstones and notes.

All his shirts have stains or tears in them, except for his fancy turquoise button up that a man from Indonesia gifted him months ago. He wears it only when we spend the night in a hostel in hopes of impressing me.

I'll admit, I'm impressed.

Especially when he eats, and eats, and eats. Come to think of it, it's quite frightening. Where does all that food go? His waist is thin and his frame is narrow. Sometimes we have unannounced eating competitions, silently wanting to out-eat the other, to be the one who consumes the most food, but I always fall below his mastery, leaving him gaping at my plate, awaiting what comes next. He reads constantly and writes with his left hand, an impression of his intelligence. When he speaks to me of other cultures, I'm always blushing, trying to hide the fact of how little I know about all the things he knows.

But nonetheless, when I ask questions he answers.

"Where have you seen the most beautiful women?"

"Oh, everywhere there are beautiful woman, except for Bolivia."

"Oh, crap. I need to go to the bathroom out here, what should I use?"

"A stick. It works better than toilet paper, trust me."

"Wait, so not all men are circumcised?"

"You really are an American, aren't you?"

Even though our voyage together has truly just begun, the fear of being cast away from Water is ever prevalent, because he is a Vagabond. Do you know what that is? Scratch those aged thoughts! A Vagabond basically translates to "someone who has nothing to lose," and in my eyes, someone who has nothing to lose is the most dangerous person in the world.

Why?

Because they quite literally have nothing to lose, nowhere to be, and no one to please. In other words, they cannot be controlled unless it is by fate alone. They are an eternal fountain of freedom. They live for themselves from moment to moment in a state of fluidity. With no plans, no projections and no desires, they go where they must, even if that means leaving others who love them behind. This is what makes them the most dangerous people in the world, but it's only frightening if you happen to love them.

So, if I continue to commit myself to being the first mate to this captain and I just so happen to get attached to his free-flowing, Vagabond spirit, what danger does that put me in? I must become like him, fully pledged to this nomadic lifestyle, by releasing the concepts of how I want my travels to turn out, so I can submerge myself completely into this wellspring of adventure.

I cannot choose to become the buoy, floating above the rolling sea at just the idea of being a Vagabond, nor do I have the option of becoming the anchor, sinking down and losing myself to this lifestyle. There is only one thing I must do.

I must become the water itself.

I must become a Vagabond alongside him.

I must become a person who has nothing to lose.

Am I willing to do this?

***

Just the two of us.

Yes.

Just the two of us.

On a rooftop in Bangkok.

Nadine is long gone, sold to another French man in Cambodia.

Jojo, Sophie, Vaidas are also long gone, their memories becoming more distant with the passing days.

My burn?

Healing well.

Nothing left but a violent violet scar upon my calf.

Tonight the sky is black, not because there is no moon to enjoy or stars to ponder at, but because the sky here in Bangkok swoops low with a polluted fog that becomes the new phenomenon. On the rooftop of our grungy new hostel, I feel I can reach up and grab at the flooded smokey haze above our crowns.

This hostel is a hole in the wall. Like a dark dungeon, it cages us in and forces us to examine the contents on its insides. Thousands of figures, images, and symbols are painted across the walls, staircase, and bathrooms, giving off the feeling you are in an enchanted video game. A purple dragon smokes a rolled-up joint alongside elves breakdancing next to a mermaid grabbing her breasts and winking at the viewer. Even the floors are painted with large compasses or splatters of color. The beaten pool table makes for a nice addition, although most of the cue sticks are broken in half.

The rooftop is caged in, in case anyone gets a bright idea, but aside from that it holds a fine atmosphere to pass the time, rest, and inquire about the perplexities of life with fellow travelers. There are old tires with pillows placed atop them to simulate a chair, a fire pit, and an aged couch that faces its front end to the street and its back end to the rooftop's staircase.

I sit with Water on this couch.

He is holding his right hand securely on his lap as he bends over it, concentrating on creating the design. We found the ink in Bangkok's China Town and the needle traveled with us from Cambodia.

"How's it coming along?"

My bewilderment is already through the (caged) roof and my impatience is growing.

"Almost done."

"I still can't believe you're doing this."

I shake my head; he doesn't respond.

An X.

Tattooed on the palm of his right hand.

Why?

Let's ask him.

"Why are you doing this again?"

"Because if I fail then I will know I'm a stupid man."

"So what if you take just one puff of a cigarette, does that count?"

He stops what he is doing and looks up at me, slightly angered.

"Dee, c'mon. You know I'm doing this to quit smoking."

His gaze returns to his project.

"I get it, but I don't understand why you have to tattoo an X on your hand to make that point."

"Because it will always remind me either of my victory or of my stupidity."

There you have it.

At this point, I am not as much in shock over the palm tattoo than at the idea of a French man quitting cigarettes.

He finishes his masterpiece and shows it to me.

I take his palm in my hand.

Through the expected stains of motor oil, dirt, and Vagabond-ness, I see it: a thin X in black ink.

I take extra care to look at his hand, making a compassionate face as I do so.

"Hey, did you know I can read palms?"

"No. I did not know this about you, but I am not surprised. You can do mine?"

"Sure, well, as I'm looking here at the crevices and lines in your palm, the first thing I see is that you, sir, are an ass. "

He pulls his tattooed hand away, snickering, which eventually simmers down to him sitting quietly on the other side of the couch, looking at me through adoring eyes. I meet his gaze and am greeted by the softness of his extraordinary mind. We both smile. Now it is I who offers my hand to him, pulling him closer by the elbow.

He slides next to me, nestling perfectly in my arms as they wrap around his narrow shoulders. I kiss the top of his head and question why he never has a bad odor. Must be a French thing, as I always stink with this heat and humidity. I can quite literally feel the waves of his mind quieting down, settling into a smooth and still bay as he absorbs my admiration.

"I still can't believe how we met."

I let his words sail past me.

"I know I'm a crazy man, I do, but I cannot help myself for this. It's hard for me, this life. There are so many things I see and want to change, so many things that hurt me—the pollution, the animals, the poverty. Sometimes I feel guilty, like I'm the one adding to these problems. I realize that when I travel in other countries I'm like a king, able to afford what I want, do as I want, and it bothers me. I want to see something different for our world, but I just don't know what to do with myself, at least not yet. I have ideas of a better way to the good life. They come from time to time and I know there is a purpose for me to be here. Many times, I almost died, Dee. Many, many times. But I'm alive still. I have been spared for something better."

He sighs, lost in thought.

"I guess I could say there is more to the reason of this tattoo on my hand. It's my commitment to be a better man, not just quitting the smoking, but changing what I eat, the resources I use, and the way I treat others. It's a commitment to go above the squawking crows in my head. They do not stop, these noises."

He looks at me, holding my hand firmer, tears just forming in the corners of his broken eyes.

"It is you who gives me hope of a better life, Dee. The way you are—you are so sweet to me. I want to be a better man for you."

He turns his head, burying it into my chest, hiding his face, hiding his tears. I hold him closer and place my cheek upon his head. I know what he feels. The pain is present in me, too. Traveling is a potent experience, as it exposes you to many things you don't expect, both good and bad. It makes you grateful and guilty all in one. It makes you question all the morals you have ever been raised on, and sometimes it hurts because you see the truth, the poverty, the suffering, and the injustice.

My heart gasps for a breath it can never consume. I close my eyes as the emotions flood me, too. How did we ever find each other in this big vast ocean of humans? So many factors could have occurred, tossing the opportunity of meeting Water right out of my life. I wonder where I would be, who I would be, if I never said yes to this adventure.

I glance down to see my left palm holding onto his right. The X startles me. I stare at it. It stares back at me. Its glare is relentless, attempting to tell me something, attempting to say:

"X marks the spot. The treasure is here."

Looks like we've both found our buried treasures.

***

The engine of the train belts out a rumbling screech as it comes to a stuttering halt.

"Dee, *allez*. This is our stop."

I look up nonchalantly, head lolling from side to side, drifting in and out of sleep.

"Allez, Deanna, we need to exit now."

I move fast, forcing myself to awaken, grabbing my bags as I drift after Water. I walk out of the train, greeting the night sky of a new town I've never been to, the familiarities of a vagabond. I absorb my surroundings and lazily notice the cast shadow that hovers in the train station. The buzzing lights blare just enough to showcase all the distant faces who wait to board the train we have just left behind.

"Shall we?" Water asks.

This means food.

It always means food.

"Yes, we shall."

Feeling like Anthony Bourdain, we make our way through the crowded town, backpacks clinging onto our sticky skin, in hopes of locating street food—fried, greasy, saucy street food. My mouth begins to salivate as our pace quickens. I can taste the MSG and soy sauce in my mouth. A bright light ahead resembles God as it shines down a golden aura onto five plastic tables alongside the road. A young Thai woman, hair plumped back in a bun, stands behind a well-equipped stall. She fries and grills, tosses and fulfills her customers' orders with a rapid speed.

Can it be true?

This late at night?

The scent lingers from her stall, entering our nostrils and summoning us like two possessed children.

We approach the chef behind the stall, but just as we open our mouths to place an order, a voice calls out from the seated plastic chairs.

"Hello! *Hello!*"

We know the voice is beckoning to us.

"Hello! Where do you come from?" it asks.

We turn around to see a middle-aged woman walking up to us, dressed fancily in a black skirt and beaded black shirt: her mourning attire for the death of King Bhumibol. She stands in front of us, smiling, eager to hear our answer.

"Oh, hello. I'm from France, and she's from the US."

"And you are traveling here?"

"Yes, we are."

"And where do you stay tonight?" she asks.

"Ah, that is a good question. We don't know yet; we've just arrived."

"Stay with me! Stay with Mama Gai. I take good care of you and I cook for you! Come."[6]

She waves her hand, asking us to follow, and begins walking away. My eyes meet his. We both shrug and continue our evening by following the short woman off into the distance, leaving behind our greasy Khai Jiao Thai omelets and the God-like light.

***

"Nakhon Sawan is number one!" Mama Gai yells over her Chang beer.[7] "Nakhon Sawan. Don't you forget it is number one, and Mama Gai loves you!"

She leans across the table to serve us more home-cooked food. We sit in the humble abode she has brought us to. It's where she feeds us, getting us drunk with her young

---

6   Translates to "Mama Chicken."

7   The beer of choice in Thailand

boyfriend late into the night. As quirky music flares from a small radio head, our beer bottles clink—another one down. Mama Gai's voice is getting louder and louder. I look to my left where Water sits with an empty plate in front of him and a puppy asleep on his lap. In the midst of nowhere, a young baby is brought to the table—Mama Gai's grandson. She places the baby into Water's arms and fills his plate up with more red curried noodles.

I cackle with Mama Gai at the scene in front of us, watching him eat with one hand and hold the baby with the other, occasionally sipping his beer.

"Get together! The two of you!" Mama Gai yells.

I squeeze next to Water and take the miraculously sleeping baby as she snaps a photo and doubles over laughing. The lights are blinking, and time begins to move in slow motion. The baby starts crying and is taken back to his mother. Water's plate is already half empty, his beer completely drained. My body is more lucid than I'd noticed earlier, and my level of alteration matches that of Mama Gai's. Her voice hasn't been getting louder, but my ears have been getting more hard of hearing.

Mama Gai grabs at my arm and brings her face close to mine, her sharp eyes piercing me. She places her pointer finger and her thumb on her chin and slowly slides them down while smiling and lifting her eyes to Water, referencing his jawline.

"Oh, he is very handsome," she flares. "You have a sexy man! Mama Gai thinks so."

Now I am doubled over laughing, the fluids inside of me taking a tumble. I look again at Water who is, incredibly, on his fourth plate of food. I notice his face and my heart palpitates. He does look strikingly handsome in this eccentric moment. Freshly shaven, his skin is defined with a gentle glisten from the sun and his cheeks are flushed in a rosy red. With his shaggy hair that waves and lands in just the perfect way, dangling loosely off the side of his head. He wears his fancy turquoise shirt which brings out the brightness in his deep-set hazel eyes. I watch his mannerisms with the puppy and the food, two things I know he adores equally.

The once-loud radio fades out in my mind. The interactions happening around me no longer matter. The beer has lost its brilliance. I gaze at Water, who does not notice my infatuation, my obsession with him. I look at him in the only way an enthralled woman can look at a man she adores. I've never been more attracted and appreciative of someone's presence in my life. In such a short amount of time he's become my best friend, my amuser, and my beloved.

Forget the Chang beer, I'm drunk off him.

My hand finds his under the table. I squeeze it once in attempt to create a bridge and pass on all the admiration I've just experienced. He looks up and smiles, squeezing my hand back. I feel the X pulsate through our flesh.

"Don't forget Nakhon Sawan is number one! Tell your friends to visit Nakhon Sawan and Mama Gai will cook for them!"

Her voice trails off.

"Nakhon Sawan!

Nakhon Sawan!

Nakhon Sawa—"

They say that if someone were to drown, they'll experience a state of ecstasy beforehand, more so than any other form of death.

Why is this?

Is it because we come from water, spending nine months in a fluid-filled sack, and it feels as if one is back in that nurturing womb?

Is it because one finally allows all the emotions they've ever suppressed to emerge?

Or is it because one needs to be in a state of danger before they can experience true love?

He is a Vagabond.

He'll never stay for long.

Please don't leave me, not quite yet.

***

We lay in bed side by side on our backs, glancing up toward the thatched ceiling and watching the fan go in circles.

"Do you remember when we built the raft in Laos?" Water asks.

The raft?

Oh yes. *The raft!*

That big goofy raft of four logs sloppily tied together. The one we had successfully used to float across a desolate pond.

"Yeah." I give a laugh of remembrance. "Of course, I remember the raft. It was an awesome day."

"Do you remember how the two girls were in the back, kicking? And Vaidas was in the front pulling the raft with a rope?"

We both laugh at this.

He continues.

"I was on the side of the raft paddling with my arm. You were standing up on the raft, tall and powerful. Looking straight out ahead, directing all of us. Your bathing suit had a nautical style, and the way it fit you was more than sexy. It was absolutely beautiful. You stood with one hand on your hip and the other hand blocking the sun from your face. You looked like the captain."

He gives an incredibly accurate description.

I can't believe he remembers that clearly.

"You remember well, don't you?" I ask.

"Yes, and I remember that I looked up from paddling and I saw you standing there, in that exact stance. It was one of the most beautiful sights I've ever seen, with the trees and water in the background, but it was the way you stood there, so bold and proud. I swear if I were an artist, I would have painted this scene on canvas."

He takes a pause.

"Deanna, that was when I fell in love with you."

I grab for his hand, turning it over in my palm while processing what he has just told me.

He's been in love with me all along.

He never planned on leaving me. The fear has been only in my head.

I hear his words again in my mind.

"That was when I fell in love with you."

He's in love with me, this Vagabond.

Did he just say that?

Where did it come from?

When my opportunity to speak comes, I avoid it and instead stay silent. I feel his hand pull away slightly. My gaze does not leave the thatched ceiling or the rotating fan. I'm too far in the depths of my mind to notice what's going on around me. I believe he's speaking to me still, but I don't hear a word.

All that lulls in my mind is the obvious fact that I've already caught the Vagabond flu, detaching myself from people, places, and things, so I can become a free spirit even more, just like him. I've been loving him with only half of me, in preparation for the potential threat of him leaving me behind. But he is not the dangerous person I have set him out to be, he *does* have something to lose, and that something is *me*.

But now I have become the Vagabond, the one I thought I needed to be.

But now the tides have turned, and I'm the most dangerous person.

For now, I have nothing to lose.

SEA OF SOULS

He wears the sad face of a clown. I look at him and I actually begin to see an imaginary mask washing away, watery tears streaming down his face. His frown imitates the crescent moon above our heads as we sit on a curb outside our hostel.

"I understand your decision, but I don't understand why it has to be like this." His breath blows in my direction, carrying with it the stale scent of whiskey.

His words are sober, yet his mind is altered from the harsh liquids.

"Why do you make this decision? I mean I understand, but I'm so upset."

It's a challenge to stay firm in my intentions, yet be compassionate toward his breaking heart, for I have my own emotions too, ones that I keep down for no one to see.

"Because I would like to travel on my own for now."

He receives my words with disbelief.

"Tell me. What is it, Dee? We have such a good time together. Have I not been good to you?"

"No, it's not that. It has nothing to do with you. I just need space. I'm sorry."

I hang my head low, heart breaking.

One thousand times he has beckoned me to just let go and fully dive in with him, but my uprising fear of crashing on solid rock has halted me from fully surrendering to Water. The depth and potential of our love has been patiently waiting underwater; he's my endearing clam and I his precious pearl.

But I just can't do it.

I don't want attachments in this Vagabond lifestyle.

To make matters more confusing, I want more than anything to surrender to him. I want to spend every day with him and grow old laughing at him, but right now is not my time to be with him.

I know it. I just know it.

I must keep moving onward.

So, I've made the hard decision to begin fending for myself. A lonely, solid rock rolling along the dusty and dry road, without Water to moisten my depleted atmosphere.

Without anything to surrender to.

Except myself.

**

We enter back into our hostel room, tears still pouring from his sad and tired eyes.

He walks in front of me and takes a seat on the bed. In his hands he holds a colorful blanket from Peru. This blanket is a sacred item, dyed royal blue with a rainbow Peruvian design threaded throughout it. I take a step closer toward him and position my tense muscles directly in front of his soft body.

"I'm sorry. I don't know why I'm so sad about this." His hands shake.

For a small moment I swallow my harshness and allow a crack of compassion to be present. I take his gentle and shivering body into my arms, his head landing just at the level of my heart. I support the back of his head in my hands, playing with his curly golden hair. As I do this, he melts into me and I into him.

Water is not an element we can easily grasp onto, yet I'm able to do so for an instant. I hold him in my arms for as long as the moment allows. He surges through and washes over me like a grand gush of movement. With this, my stone-like frame of mind delicately cracks and a single tear streams out of my right eye.

I feel like I'm alive.

He frees his body from my tight grasp and looks up at me.

"I traveled with this blanket for seven years. It's my favorite thing I own, but you are more important to me than anything. I want you to have it. "

My lips frown as I hesitantly take the gift from his outstretched arms.

"I love you, Dee."

***

I stand grounded on the tall balcony, with the room we slept in last night and all of its history encased behind me. I wear a long, floral skirt gifted to me by a Burmese man. It quivers in the eerie breeze. My gaze lowers as I watch the fading frame of the man I love. His vintage pack hangs upon his shoulders, his feet move with a mission, a mission I, and only I, have given him: the mission to walk away from me.

I know it right here and now, as I stand peacefully on this balcony watching the scene pan out. I've been in this moment many, many times before, throughout multiple lifetimes and fitted in an array of different scenarios. There I am standing calmly above, watching him voyage off into the distance—off to war, off to discover, off to transcend the seven seas. He's had many roles throughout his lifetimes—a messenger, a religious figure, a warrior, a botanist.

Yet I notice while his role stretches far and wide across these varied scenarios, my role casually and permanently stays the same: the peaceful presence of a woman always watching him from above, blessing him on his journey ahead, knowing deep down in my heart that, although I love him, to make him stay alongside me would shatter his soul. It would be like trying to block the ocean from shifting tides.

It is not my place.

He is a Great Voyager, and he must always be in flow, just like me.

***

A raven comes to me in my dreams tonight. At first, he pierces me with his beady, black, little eyes, communicating that he is far more powerful than I am. I remain silent and simply listen to what he has to share.

He begins:

"You will see me once and never again. I'm the raven spirit and I appear only when there is a spirit who needs to have a keen eye kept on them from birth onward, for they cannot do so themselves, for they roam wildly.

"You see, on Earth every spirit is connected in a multitude of ways. Like the ocean in one location, many millions of droplets create the entirety of the sea across this planet. Each drop of water is constantly in communication through an energetic pulse, an electrical synapse.

"The same goes for humankind. Each person adds to the masses a unique drop, creating an ocean of spirits who are constantly in some form of communication, whether they know it or not. They synchronize, ebb and flow, teach each other, learn from each other, and show each other how they're all connected, how they are all one.

"Sometimes when you meet someone, it's not possible to have foresight of the magnitude their presence will have on your life or your journey ahead. For you humans, it may take time, years even, for you to realize why certain people come and go. This is the case with you and your beloved Water. You come from the same constellation, holding similar visions for this planet.

"I've played a big role in what connects the two of you, sent to look after him but guiding you to ensure the crossing of your paths. It is to my surprise that you have made the decision to leave him, as you two are a pair of soulmates and have joyfully anticipated the moment of being together once again in human form.

"You have left him with a fallen heart, broken and emotional. I must stay true to my duties and return to him. Since you chose to leave him, it brings an end to the agreement between you and I. Goodbye."

The raven stops speaking and blinks once, twice, but before he blinks a third time, I call out to him in a panic, needing to know one last thing.

"Raven, wait!"

"What?"

"Please tell me. What constellation do we come from, him and I?"

"Canis Major. You Adhara and him Sirius, and his name, the one you cannot pronounce, means 'Bright Raven,' hence my presence."

With that thought the raven blinks his third blink, spreads his mighty wings, and leaves me in a flash.

I'm no longer dreaming the same scene, but now standing in the center of a sea, a sea of human spirits who are coming and going, ebbing and flowing, living and dying. Altogether they create a synchronization of souls though their personal stories, making their journeys here on planet Earth as unique as my own.

***

The first lesson of Water is the lesson of connection. We are all connected after all, whether you believe it or not. You heard the raven spirit, didn't you? We're a sea of souls, an ocean of spirits, a wellspring of human beings. We push up against one another as close as two tiny droplets possibly can, and before we know it, we are suddenly cast out so far from each other to possibly never cross tides again. It is connection which helps us catalyze one another, sparking off divine opportunities for growth and evolution.

The second lesson of Water is the lesson of intuition. Water asks us to be intuitive. Before you enter the waves, you must first stand away from them and take the time to observe their rhythm, bringing yourself to know the patterns of the ocean's movements. The same can be said of our emotions, which hold the key to our intuition. We must take a step back to watch our inner waves rise and fall so we can make the most compassionate and intentional decisions for everyone involved. If we fail to take the time and make observations, we may make rash decisions which leave traces of pain in our hearts and the hearts of others.

The third lesson of Water is the lesson of surrender. At times certain treasures come to greet us in our lives, though they may at first be disguised. We need to see them for what they are and drop the connotations that we project onto them. How can we be delighted by a gift if we are already making speculations at what it is or could offer us? Water is always in flow, asking you to trust the divinity of what is being offered with hopes you will surrender to the buried treasure when it is marked with an X right in front of you.

***

I awake with a start, sitting up in my bed, heart racing and throat dry. I look around the room, searching for his large backpack thrown on the floor. I don't see it. I pat the bed, feeling for his calloused hand. I don't feel it. I quiet my breathing, listening for his silent snores. I don't hear them.

I lean back into my pillow, and as I do my eyes catch sight of the Peruvian blanket he gifted me. Without warning it all comes back: the conversation, the view off the balcony, the dream of the raven.

Like a tsunami of great and forceful emotions, it hits me.

He is a Vagabond. He has no phone and no email address.

Not to mention, I never did learn how to say his name.

I bring the blanket to my face. Tears begin to stroll down my cheeks as I mourn the drought to come.

The absence of Water.

Modeling for a mock wedding at the Dirty Shack with Air.
Photo credit Allie Frank.

Surf time with Janet and Air.

Working the counter at Gypsea Gelato.

Hitchhiking with Water through Thailand. Picked up by a
group of police officers.

Twenty minutes after the first burn and four shots of LaoLao.

Nadine and the Great Explorer.

Earth lighting up a smoke with Maximón in a hotel room.

The Jester and the Princess.

Enjoying a lollipop while in Southern Mexico.

The man with a box of books sharing insights with Fire. Photo credit Michelle Feathers.

Bountiful Harvest. Photo Credit Michelle Feathers.

EARTH

THE FORGOTTEN CHILD

———

Two young Spider monkeys leap to-and-fro, high atop the canopies of the profound, mysterious, and unfaltering Guatemalan jungle.

Past the winding waterfalls of Semuc Champey, with its hundreds of tourists. Past Flores, the shrinking town that floats casually over Lake Petén, and way past Tikal, whose mesmerizing structure holds little of the magic it once did. Fit snuggly against its cousins Chiapas and Belize, the Guatemalan jungle stands tall and magnificent despite humans' incomprehensible need to destroy beautiful things.

"Catch me, ya rat face!" the sister monkey calls out to her brother.

"You're as slow as a swamped-out crocodile!" he hollers, propelling himself forward with his mighty tail.

Up and down, they swing their awkwardly long and furry arms, gripping branch after branch until they happen upon a tree, and not just any tree. This tree is a golden gift, presenting its deliciously ripe fruit the way an elder monkey would present the purest form of honey to her fellow tribe. The mamey sapote fruits on the tree are certainly ripe and ready to be consumed by any lucky chap who happens to find its delight.

"Woah," both young Spider monkeys gawk in unison, "*so much sapote.*"

Just as the young ones reach their delighted and sweaty palms out toward the ripest fruit of the branch, an almighty sound, rooted and robust, belches out across the landscape. Its vibrating tone roars ferociously, captivating all ears, whether amphibian, mammal, bird, or reptile, that hears its blow.

The young Spider monkeys freeze like porcelain dolls, staying completely still in bewilderment during the entirety of the sound. No one can tell how long the noise persists because no one counts time in the jungle, but once the noise comes to a halt the young Spider monkeys release their grip around the precious sapote they hold in their palms, letting them smash onto the jungle floor below.

The young monkeys look at each other, eyes wide in oblivion, until a second wave of cacophony comes roaring like a ripple of thunder, rushing from all corners of the jungle that surrounds them.

Through the sporadic squawks of many birds—Toucans, Vultures, and Quetzals. Through the slithering and slippery tones of hundreds of snakes: Corals, Puffing Snakes, Green Vines, and Milk Snakes. Through the protruding moans of herds of mammals: Tapirs, Pacas, and Coatimundi.

They all seem to be saying the same thing.

"The horn," screech the birds.

"The horn," hiss the snakes.

"The horn," grumble the mammals.

The Spider monkeys, still locked in eye contact, state aloud at precisely the same time in a whispered voice, "The horn."

Now, you may find this event rather odd—bizarre, perhaps—but let me assure you that every creature in the Guatemalan Jungle, no matter what shape, size, color, coating, method of transportation, age, or race knows of this horn and the purpose behind it. To obey the horn is both an instinct and agreement within the spirit of all animals who live in this jungle, for whenever the horn is blown, they are to come and gather around the base of the World Tree.

Who blew the horn?

Well, Quetzalcoatl of course.

Given the utmost respect, Quetzalcoatl, the Mayan god who connects the realm of the Earth to the realm of the sky, is summoning all creatures to gather. Creatures of the Earth—animals, insects and plant spirits—and creatures of the skies—gods, goddesses, and saints—are in the process of joining, as they do every year, in honor of the winter solstice.

During this gathering located at the base of the World Tree, all beings will join in harmony with one another, work out any injustices, discuss humanity's current crisis and envision peace for the year to come. It's a respectable event, one only the Mayan god of creation can declare. No humans have been allowed since "the disconnect," which is rarely discussed these days.

So, we will not discuss it.

***

Gasping for air, yet moving as quickly as only Spider monkeys can, the brother and sister stop for a rest on a tall branch. All around them the other animals surge forward in their fast-paced migration, for right up ahead stands the destination these creatures have in mind: the World Tree. It's the first time these young ones will see such a gathering, and the spectacle they observe now gives off quite a euphoric feeling.

Colors spew from every angle, not just Earthly colors, but the colors of gods—the colors most humans are, unfortunately, blind to. They shift and sway around the World Tree like magnetic rainbows of the universe. Thousands and thousands of creatures, both fearsome and adorable, have encircled themselves in an orderly fashion, standing attentive to what awaits. It's a sight that reminds one of the ultimate magic of the jungle, the mysteriousness.

A hum begins to emanate from all beings as they bow their loyal heads to Quetzalcoatl.

The Spider monkeys weave their way to the center, taking their instinctual place among the crowd, which resides neck and neck with the Howler monkeys and the Capuchin monkeys.

"What's going on?" they whisper to their neighbor.

"Quetzalcoatl is assigning spirit animals!" the Howler monkey screeches with such ferocity it shakes the air.

"Spirit animals?"

"YES!" the Howler screams again. "You know, to protect those crazy fools, *those humans!*"

Every animal in the encompassing circle now turns and looks at the Howler monkey, whose naturally loud voice has created a scene. This is typical for a Howler monkey, as they have a hard time remaining quiet. But because of this disturbance, this scene, Quetzalcoatl brings his speech to a dramatic halt and turns toward the chaos amongst them.

He rises tall from his throne in the way only a feathered-serpent god can do and begins to make his way toward the commotion.

Step by step, the animals nervously part to allow the grandiose god to walk by, section by section, weaving through lizards, snakes, birds, ocelots, frogs, and primates until his gaze falls directly upon the two young Spider monkeys. The immensely magnificent feather headdress he wears upon his crown blocks the rays of sun from blinding the two monkeys, who ogle, wide-mouthed, at Quetzalcoatl.

Silence permeates the spectacle for many long moments. Not even a croak from a frog, flap from a bird, or snicker from a goddess is made until Quetzalcoatl finally breaks it by summoning a smirk upon his face.

"I won't hurt you, little ones. In fact, I want to make peace. I find it rather brave, perhaps, that you young ones were talking during the most vital annual ceremony in all of the jungle."

The Spider monkeys swallow a big gulp, but don't say a word; they cannot not say a word.

"Follow me, young ones. I will take you to Grandfather. C'mon, right this way." Quetzalcoatl turns swiftly on his heel and walks with celestial confidence back the same way he came.

For a moment, the young Spider monkeys stay in place, not knowing what to do, until they are nudged from behind by an ocelot. The brother and sister glare at one another and follow the path the god walks before them.

***

Around the other side of the World Tree is a large opening in which the monkeys follow Quetzalcoatl into. The inside is dark, yet a subtle flow exists due to the many lit candles encircling an eye-catching altar. A strange, odorous smoke greets the tiny nostrils of the two young Spider monkeys and makes them sneeze on command.

The god graces right up to a hidden figure who sits among the shadows. The figure's shape is easily seen despite the lackluster lighting, revealing the frame of an old man: Grandfather, the one known as Maximón. This man, dressed completely in black, wears a large sombrero over his head so that no features of his face can be seen—just the low-lit cigarette hanging loosely out the brim of his lips. His gaze is facing downward, forever staring at the earth and his wrists and ankles are tied with twine to the chair upon which he sits.

"Monkeys, meet Maximón. Maximón, meet monkeys. These young ones were talking during our ceremony, and I trust you will assign them properly. I must go now." Quetzalcoatl, about to return to his previous importance, bows his head and exposes more of the elaborate headdress he wears. On the way out of the hollowed trunk, he turns around just to add a brief clarification.

"Do remember young ones: this is not a punishment. It is, how do you say...a privilege. Enjoy."

With that, the Spider monkeys are left alone in the hollowed-out passageway of the World Tree, staring at an old saint tied to a chair surrounded by candles, bottles of alcohol, and cigarettes.

After many awkward moments of silence, the old man coughs a few hard times and then clears his throat to speak.

"Light me up, would ya?"

The monkeys stand still, completely clueless to the needs of Maximón.

"The candle to the cigarette. Hurry up, would ya? I'm dying in this chair!" he grunts.

The monkeys move fast, placing a fresh cigarette into the old saint's mouth, lighting it with a burning candle.

"Great. Now, where were we? Oh. Si, si." Maximón grins at his own inner thoughts and shifts slightly in his tied chair.

"Assignment, si."

His tone is anything but amusing, yet it's not angry either. It's just right in the middle. He speaks only when he must, delivering the information and leaving little room for questioning.

"You have been assigned. Si, assigned to, how should I say?" Maximón puffs as he ponders for a moment. "Be a guide for a young human man. He is sort of a stray cat, if you will. He lives in Guatemala City, very far from here."

"You see, the boy is troubled," Maximón coughs loudly and continues, "he's not even two decades old and has already committed many wrongdoings. It's not his fault. It's only, ugh..." a brief pause, "his karmic path or something like that."

If Maximón were to have his hands untied, he would've used them to wave around indifferently during this statement.

"Born to the streets of what they call 'the ghetto,' his life has been rather sad, dangerous, and difficult, to say the least." Maximón puffs away.

"With a life of constant hardships that falls upon his shoulders, this young man has been left without a supportive family. So, do you know what he has decided to do? The only option left for a stray cat in the ghetto. He has taken to the streets, where his choices have become ill-advised and reckless. He will soon destroy himself or get killed in the process of destruction itself. But either way, he needs a change, or maybe just an ounce of hope, and he needs to come back to the earth where he belongs."

Maximón stops what he is saying and brings his gaze toward an open bottle of tequila on the floor. He then glances back at the two young Spider monkeys who stand frozen, completely absorbed by the whole occurrence thus far.

"Would ya? Do ya mind? Pour me some damn tequila, could ya?"

At this, the Spider monkeys move as quickly as ever, pouring the rest of the tequila bottle into the old saint's mouth.

"*Que rico.*" Maximón settles further with a soft grin upon his face.[8]

"So, there you have it. This challenged young man, let's just say he needs some help. He's a forgotten child of the earth, a lost child of the jungle, with limitless potential and a wellspring of creativity, but he is born and bound to the streets of the city. If no one is assigned to look over him, then it would be too easy for his whole life to pass by without a reconnection to the spirit of the land, his *Tierra*. It's the place where his soul has the chance to come alive, in hopes of healing from him traumatic early life.

"You need to guide him away from the city and its danger, and closer toward the jungle, so that he can heal his heart from all this ill fate."

At this, Maximón finishes his spell and falls asleep rather immediately, still completely bound in the chair, his head dangling even more downward.

---

8   How delicious

The brother and sister Spider monkey are now left extraordinarily confused in the absence of Maximón's words. How on Quetzalcoatl's creation can they help this Forgotten Child?

In a fit of bravery, the brother steps forward with courage enough to ask the old saint a rather necessary question.

"Maximón, sir, how can we help this Forgotten Child? He's so far away, and we are rather...young and inexperienced monkeys and, well, animal guides at that."

The old saint awakens enough to hear the meek voice, and for the first time his eyes meet the eyes of the young monkeys before him. In his listless heart, he begins to feel a pang of rawness, of compassion, for these young ones who are totally inexperienced and naive. The task which has been put upon them is a rather challenging one, strange and daunting to say the least.

Maximón sighs, showing his compassion outwardly for the first time in eons.

"The best ways to help him, young ones, is through his dreams. Get straight to the point. It's in the astral realm and through imagination where ancestors, animal spirits, and guides of all sorts connect with the 'disconnected' consciousness of humans. You are animal, and so you are born with this already in your blood, *and*," Maximón stops, grins, and looks mischievously around, "in the rhythm of music. You can send messages influencing him through the vibrations of any music that enters his ears. Close your eyes and whisper to him. He will hear. I promise, he will. Though his brain may not consciously know it, his spirit will get the message. You got it, young ones? *Si? Todo bien?*"

Before the monkeys could reply, Maximón falls sound asleep again.

They turn their gaze toward one another, still utterly perplexed but willing to give this dream guidance thing a try. They shrug and grab each other's paws and lace their tails, creating a bridge over their heads. The saint was right; this instinct is already in their blood! They close their eyes, and with intentions they begin to speak and whisper to the Forgotten Child.

"Come home, child, come home. Heal your heart and come home to *Pachamama*."

They both imagine a vine growing from where they stand and weaving its way throughout the rolling jungle, past the abandoned ruins, until it reaches the ominous streets of Guatemala City where a young man stops right in his tracks. He places a hand over his heart which begins to beat furiously, nearly palpitating out of his chest.

***

The young man is frightened, as this racing of the heart has never occurred, especially not without reason. He is a tough guy, so why should his heart react in a way such as this?

Treacherous things he has witnessed, and even more treacherous things he has done, not out of violence but out of fear. He did it out of a fear of being rejected, of being abandoned, as it seems to have been the theme of his life thus far.

His oldest brother abandoned him on the day he was shot twice during his friend's wedding. His father abandoned him when he guzzled down one too many and left the family unaided. His childhood sweetheart abandoned him in hopes of pursuing her schooling. His mother abandoned him to work day and night, trying as hard as she could to feed the four other mouths at home.

Now, as he stands on the sidewalk in the center of the city, his heart racing and not showing signs of giving up anytime soon, his awareness is caught in a most interesting way. With clarity, he sees it all: his longing to live does not reside in his commitment to his brotherhood, but in his desire to make music and the curiosities of traveling.

Without thinking, he finds himself walking to an outdoor market. Out of his pockets, he pulls a couple of bills. He purchases three things: a hair crochet needle, a small blue boombox, and a camouflage backpack.

Within the week, he kisses his mother goodbye, begins to style his hair into dreads, and pursues his newfound lifestyle away from the city.

All while making the most of what he has.

All while staying alive.

ONCE UPON A BUS

I pick my head up, eyes squinting competitively. I lock contact with the sight before me. I look into their eyes, one by one. Then my gaze shifts downward, toward their breasts, their wet, protruding breasts, spewing water like mother's milk, beckoning me to stay longer, if only just for a moment to quench my thirst through sight alone. The water flows downward and piles up in a basin below. The sweat on my neck builds up. I want to reach my hand out and touch them.

The breasts.

Just one.

Just to get my fingers wet.

I take a step closer and extend my arm, offering myself while asking to be offered to.

My skin grazes past the tarnished metal, and my hand soaks in old fountain water.

"Señora..."

I keep my hand pressed against the statue, feeling the subtle coolness deliver itself to the rest of my body.

"Excuse me, señora."

I close my eyes and stand frozen.

"Señora. ¿*Todo bien?*"[9]

My eyelids lift to see a middle-aged man standing right next to me, watching me fondle the voluptuous breast of a tarnished water fountain sculpture. I see the concern on his face, as my whole arm is dripping wet. I slowly pull away, wiping my arm across my forehead without breaking eye contact with him.

"*Si. Todo bien.*"

I pick up my backpack and observe the commotion in Central Park.

Antigua, Guatemala.

A city that comes alive in the morning, stays alive all throughout the day, and continues its fortitude well into the night-time. When the sun drops behind the distant landscape, tourists from every corner of the city crawl out of their hostels like well-dressed vampires with cash in hand. They sweep past the nightclubs and free salsa classes, amusing themselves with child's play and tequila. Argentineans leading the masses.

Colorful pastel buildings stand tall over the cobblestone streets but are constantly threatened by the highly active volcanos that stand taller over them. In the depths of the night, during a common clear sky, you may just see the hyper red lava and the curling grey fumes erupting from Vulcan De Fuego, and when this happens you may also just be lucky enough to hear a round of applause coming from a distant rooftop. Argentineans once again.

You can find anything here, from little voodoo dolls, to fried pork liver, to old men who dance better than most young women. I experienced this delicacy on my second night when

---

9   Miss, everything okay?

a man well over the age of my father twirled me around like a lifeless doll at a salsa club. His hand had started on my hip and by the middle of the song it migrated elsewhere. When the song ended, he dipped me low and brought his sterling face to mine. "You are an incredibly sexy woman."

Antigua is indescribable. There's a luminance to it that makes you question if you are finally living or if you have finally died. It's a good place to be if you want something unique to happen to you without putting in much effort. Earlier this week I was cursed at by a half-blind woman when I didn't purchase a molded papaya off her. And just today I stood witness to a mad man reciting a poem to the pigeons in Central Park. I quickly became his one and only spectator, as the pigeons flew away after the first verse.

See, these are the types of things you experience when you open yourself up—things which don't actually mean anything at all and never will. But they become like memory gems, stored in the back pocket of the mind and pulled out at any time for amusing reminiscing.

I adore Antigua because it adores me.

My first month in Latin America, and I still have all my organs.

Hallelujah.

The fountain ladies in front of me have not stopped spewing water from their metal breasts, and the man standing beside me is still standing beside me. Maybe he's no longer concerned about my well-being, but rather concerned about my relationship status.

I return my gaze to him.

"*Eres muy, muy bonita.*"[10]

---

10   You are very beautiful.

That's my cue to leave. I pick up my pack and strap it on. My mouth is parched from a combination of the hot sun and a fever that decided today was the perfect day to be born. With my backpack slumped on and in a stoic state, I push past the man and work my way through the crowd, continuing onward to my new home for the next month.

I nearly miss it—the hole in the wall. I have to backtrack five paces and check the name painted across the dilapidated building. Apparently, this is the hostel I signed up for. The second I walk through the doorway my fever intensifies, and my legs get weaker, threatening to face-plant me. I place my palms on the glass desk in a desperate manner, slide my passport across the table, and snatch the keys to my room.

Scurrying up the staircase, I bump from wall to wall like a drunk Australian until I reach room 216. I thrust the key into the lock, thrust the door open, and throw myself onto the bed. Under the covers my body shakes, vibrates, and aches, locking me in a chokehold and freezing me into a dark corner of dreary slumber.

It's a slumber that lasts twelve hours.

I dream of the water fountain, the breasts, and the tarnished metal.

They melt before my eyes, leaving me with nothing except the ground that I stand upon.

***

The light never comes, and it takes me a moment to realize why. There is none. It's night-time. I've slept through the entire day. I give a little stretch under the covers, feeling the pool of sweat I've created in my deep slumber. The clock says 8:30 p.m., but my stomach says "now." That's a demand. I stand, stretch, and reach for a few bills. As I'm folding them to stuff down my bra, I hear a bolt of laughter.

"That's nice," I think aloud.

The laughter happens again.

I can hear it, clearer.

Like an invisible light, it pulls me out of my vault and guides me down the stairs from which I came twelve hours earlier. On the last step I am greeted by a fluorescent light hanging over the only counter in the café and three sets of eyes gathered around it. All are staring at me. Apparently I've disrupted their conversation, as the laughter vanishes the moment I slide onto a stool.

The young man behind the counter recognizes me from earlier.

"Where have you been all day?"

"Resting. I didn't feel good, but must've slept it off."

"You've got more than the travel bug. You probably want to eat something, right?"

I look at him as if he is God himself.

"Yes. Yes, I would."

"I got you, *chica*."

He turns the fryer on and starts dicing away.

One down, two more to go. I can still feel their eyes on me, waiting to introduce themselves or be introduced to. I take a deep breath, my last one, before forcing myself to transform into a social butterfly. When my gaze finally lifts, it meets the eyes of a smiling Korean woman.

"And how are you today?" my voice croaks out.

"Good. These guys are teaching me Spanish."

"Oh yeah," I can already see the naivety soaking through her shirt, bringing me back to the image of the fountain. "What exactly are you learning?"

"They are teaching me slang. *Cerote*."

The two others in the room explode laughing with the mention of this word.

Sounds like I need a lesson.

"What does it mean?"

The young man behind the counter breaks in.

"It can be a really offensive term, like how you would call someone a jackass in English. But you can also use it in the context of 'homie.' By the way, my name is Alex."

"My name is Sohyun," the Korean woman chimes in.

"Nice to meet you both. I'm Deanna."

I feel the third and final set of eyes penetrating my right profile, sitting just beside me. I've yet to fully notice him until now, when he finally speaks.

"Hell-o."

I smile skeptically and bow my head, not offering him anything further.

"Nice to meet you," he speaks again.

"And who are you?"

His gaze does not waver but remains in full spotlight directly on top of my face. He answers my question by keeping quiet and smiling, on the verge of laughter, mocking me.

"Deanna," Alex calls from behind the counter. "He doesn't speak English. Well, he knows a few words but not enough to understand you."

"Oh, my bad."

"*Que dice?*"[11] The young man beside me speaks in quick Spanish to Alex. Together they laugh, causing me to blush because god only knows what they're saying. The two of them are so provocative in just the way they are speaking, not to

---

11   What is she saying?

mention their mannerisms and coincidental good looks. I'm not sure which one I'd prefer. My gaze goes back and forth to both in an attempt to find a conclusion to this inquiry.

My fantasy is brought to a halt when Alex turns the spotlight onto me.

"He wants you to go with him tomorrow on the buses."

"The buses?"

"Yeah, it's where he works."

"What?" I laugh in judgment. "What does that even mean?"

"You'll see, just go with him tomorrow."

I glance to my right to see the same mysterious eyes still parked on my face. His smile is pushing up against me like the Cheshire Cat, making me question the intentions behind it and making me also question my own intentions. For the first time, I take deeper notice of his features. His skin is caramel in color, smooth, youthful, and brilliant. He's young, I believe, but confident in his immaturity, which we all know is immaturity on its worst behavior. Over his stocky shoulders hang his loose dreads, adorned with beads, colored string, and charms. His eyebrows raise and lower, enticing me further to join him tomorrow.

He looks like a real-life voodoo doll, a cute one.

I think he is the one I would choose.

Sorry, Alex. You're not too bad yourself, though.

The voodoo doll replaces any chance of a normal first impression by standing up and pulling a blue boombox out of an old backpack.

"*Escucha.*"[12]

The young man proceeds to plug in his phone and selects a song with a rhythmic beat and fat bass. He clears his throat,

---

12 Listen

eager to deliver what was clearly never ordered. Sharp and without warning come words like bullets, fast shooting and boisterous. The words contain plenty of rhymes, none of which I comprehend because I'm a white girl from New Jersey. The syllables of Spanish words fly out and twist around like bats out of hell, encircling me with charisma and asking for a competition.

I see it for what it is: a rap battle.

No longer do my ailments and aches exists. They have all but vanished in honor of the adrenaline this situation has conjured. I stand up, grin matching his, and the second he completes his lyrical mastery I deliver mine. I throw words at him in English that he will never understand, nor would he even want to. I allow my Jersey accent to slide a little more than usual, catching the flow on fire with brash insults and clumsy poetry. Everyone's attention is on me—even the eggplant that's in frying in the pan. I can feel it. His Cheshire smile drops, with good reason, as I lay out my last line in the only Spanish I know.

"*Tal vez soy una gringa, pero eres una puta.*"

The beat stops, my mind eases, and I take a seat and begin to eat the eggplant sandwich which has magically appeared in front of me. I'll take it as a reward for my accomplishment.

I won the battle.

What proceeds is silence. No one has anything to say, not even I, the victorious, until my meal is interrupted by the sound of a throat clearing. My periphery alerts me of an outstretched caramel arm.

"*Mucho gusto.*"

"Nice to meet you too."

I've made contact with Earth.

***

My dusty shoes pound on the uneven ground as I follow behind my new friend, while skepticism hovers around me. He doesn't stop singing. In fact, he never shuts up. Like a parrot, a monkey, and a rooster all in one, the many noises escaping from his mouth leave me occasionally entertained yet mostly annoyed.

"Da da da, da da do. *Hola Nena.*"

He's flirtatious. Let's not forget where we are here: in a land where *no* woman would have any issue conceiving.

I won't lie now. After my victory in the rap battle, I've been wearing the title like a crown and paying little attention to my Jester opponent. He's had to be effortful in his attempts of speaking with me and creative in his invitations. I'll admit, I finally broke today when he took off a colorful scarf from his neck and tied it around my head.

"*Que bonita, Nena. Ahora vamos.*"[13]

He grabbed my elbow and pulled me out of the hostel with him.

Apparently, I need to be more creative in my methods of saying yes.

We are walking faster now, and the uneven sidewalk threatens to break my ankle with every other step. My shoulder nearly slams into protruding doors and caged-in windows with each corner we turn. I keep my hands in my pockets and my shoulders down, letting the world know that I am *cool*. Out of the corner of my eye I see him glancing at me, still wearing that ridiculous grin upon his face.

Is this guy always this happy?

---

13   How beautiful, babe. Now let's go.

"*Tan linda, Nena.*"[14]

It's like he can read my mind. Dammit.

He sees my face and now he belts out laughing.

We approach an open plaza where teenagers are getting frisky and children are playing with a deflated soccer ball. Earth's body comes to a knowing halt with ease, as if he's done this a thousand times before. He slips off his torn backpack and takes the boombox out.

"*Esperamos aquí, Nena.*"[15]

I take his cue.

"*Bueno.*"

We wait for ten minutes with the boombox billowing, which draws even more attention our way. He's still chanting lyrics under his breath, grooving his body on the sidewalk in front of everyone. I'm blushing as the locals look from him to me, then back again. I don't want to hear the thoughts inside their minds. Earth casually peeks his head down the street, noticing a colorful bus heading our way. It's a large hunk of metal, an old school bus painted with sinfully clashing colors, all while spewing black exhaust.

It's a "chicken bus," a term phrased for the local buses that take passengers all around Guatemala and throughout the cities. Chicken buses have acquired their name from travelers who have found it a comical scene to walk onto a bus with people, luggage, and clucking chickens in cages. Apparently they enjoyed this scene, and thus the name was coined.

"*¿Lista, Nena?*"

I understand that.

"Yes, I'm ready."

---

14   So cute, babe.

15   Let's wait here.

I enter the bus first as he holds his boombox up from behind me, voicing to the driver: *"Aye! Permiso hermano."*[16]

The driver sees him, hears him, and acknowledges him, but doesn't say a word. Instead, he nods his head in a minimalistic way, giving permission for his passengers to be entertained.

I swing into a seat directly in the middle of the elongated bus, sitting alongside a local woman who carries a basket of over two hundred eggs. My eyes are glued to him now as he increases the volume of his voice and introduces himself. He's certainly a Jester. His dreadlocks are bobbing up and down as the bus bumps its way through the ancient city. That smile is *still* there.

Without haste, he turns on his beat and, just like he did in the hostel, his performance commences. The words fly out of his mouth again, pounding the ears of the passengers. I'm slightly mortified. Who would do such a thing? But as I look around me, I see the faces of everyone else, and they are smiling.

Just like him.

The children have stopped fighting with their siblings to stare open-mouthed at him. The grandmothers with long silver braids clutch their market goods and show their worn teeth. The middle-aged men with tight blue jeans and cowboy boots hide behind their mustaches, leaving their phones untouched on their laps.

I'm in awe. He's captivated the whole bus, including myself.

Who's the Jester now?

What he does next surprises me—or rather, what happens next. Everyone's going into their bags, coin purses, and

---

16 Permission brother.

pockets to dig out cash, pure Guatemalan cash. Little colorful bills with birds on them, centavos with flowers, and Mayan faces. I watch as Earth, still smiling, walks up and down the bus, collecting his salary. He makes eye contact with each person he passes, bowing his head in sincere gratitude.

I feel a hand tap me on the shoulder in the middle of my memorization.

"*Vamos, Nena.*"

I stand up and he escorts me off the bus.

Now I'm the one smiling bigger than him, impressed to say the least.

The Jester has entertained the Princess.

My smile glares as I watch him count his earnings.

I count along with him.

Seventy Quetzals.[17]

He just made ten dollars in two minutes, which is more than I've ever made for a performance of my own.

He notices my face now and he is further delighted.

"*Te gusto, Nena?*"[18]

"*Si! Mucho.*"

I can't help but to nod like a fool. Not to mention it's literally all I can say, for my Spanish lacks the words "awesome," "interesting," "dope," and "impressive."

"*Gracias, gracias, Nena. ¿Otra vez?*"[19]

Just as he asks, another bus pulls up directly in front of us.

God, spirit, or whatever you call it has a funny way of sending messages, huh?

---

17 Guatemalan currency

18 Did you like it babe?

19 Thank you thank you babe, again?

Before I have time to answer, I hear the word *"permiso"* and feel a hand pushing me forward.

***

We're nearing the end of the bus route, just about to pull into Antigua's large marketplace. I begin to recognize my surroundings again, but I'm in a different world, no longer uptight and stoic but entertained and relaxed. My perspective has been altered by the Jester who is collecting his coins once again. I wait for him, and when the bus parks we both land our feet on the dusty floor of the parking lot.

The people here are on a mission, but they're in no rush whatsoever. The good life of Latin America, where everyone has a place to be, but they don't have a time they need to be there. They carry baskets of produce atop their heads, with chickens in cages and bags of clothing. The colors alone are enough for an enchantment.

"Sígueme."[20]

Earth grabs my arm and pulls me forward with his never-ending confidence, leaving my distracting thoughts behind.

A cat and mouse chase begins. He weaves past the venders, and I follow. He sinks below the rusted structures and pipes, and I follow. He slides his way between the crowds of people, and I follow. We move fast, on a mission, and my eyes catch hold of every fruit and produce vender, and when they see me they stand up and beckon me to come closer. It's a challenge to not abide.

Finally, we stop at none other than a peanut vendor.

Yes, a peanut vendor.

---

20 Follow me

A person selling peanuts from two-hundred-pound bags. You can get the raw peanuts or the shelled peanuts. You have the option of toasted or salted. Would you, señora, perhaps like to try our chili lime peanuts? Or how about our cinnamon-sugar peanuts? And just for good measure, we also offer pistachios for those with a more cultured palette.

Earth pulls a single bill from his pocket and places his order. The vender hands him a bag of salted peanuts all while laughing at my astonished face. He passes the bag on to me as if I were the one who asked for it and slips the change into his pocket.

"*Vamos.*"

He's back to moving at a confident pace. I'm back to following him, holding onto the peanuts like a precious child.

I open the bag and pop a few in my mouth. Hey, these aren't so bad. In fact, I forgot how damn delicious peanuts are. I'm instantaneously addicted, shoving the peanuts into my mouth faster than I can swallow and chew. This is the best way salted peanuts can be eaten: like a slob while walking through a large outdoor marketplace in Guatemala. Mr. Peanut would be proud. Earth glances behind him to witness my efforts and laughs endlessly, pleased that he has delighted the Princess yet again.

"*¿Te gusta, Gordita?*"[21]

There is no time to answer, only time to taste the salt on my tongue, which is actually a perfect answer to his question.

We push ourselves through the market and out onto the cobblestone streets of Antigua. The bright sunshine dazes us for only a moment before our pace picks up again. This time we're skipping, running like gleeful fools through the streets,

---

21 Do you like it, chubby?

past the cars, past the police officers, and past the stray dogs that want a peanut.

I grab a handful of the nuts and, instead of shoving them into my mouth, I decide to share by tossing them, one at a time, toward Earth. He catches a few in his mouth and holds his stomach, laughing. Peanuts are flying everywhere, my flip flops are coming off, everyone is staring at us as humor aids our charades.

Our laughter is not sustained on words, stories, or inside jokes. Little dialogue is exchanged, just actions and observations. I can't speak his language and he can't speak mine, but what we're experiencing is more brilliant than any spoken language. It's the pure interaction of two human beings having a hell of a good time by just simply being, like children.

I suppose this is how the Jester makes himself known—through motions and movements, entertainment and smiles. His silly ways have certainly caught my attention. He's grounded and real—a real-life human with a real-life personality. He just does what he wants and brings joy to the lives of others, me now included.

How fun it is to know the Jester, whose constant smile is highly contagious, highly attractive, and potentially dangerous.

We reach the hostel with a quick halt, bag of peanuts empty, huddled over with hands on each other's back. Like two tall trees that don't have the ability to speak yet know the secrets of the forest, we look each other directly in the eyes and silently plant our first precious interaction together underground.

THE SAINT OF SIN

For the past week the schedule of my daily routine goes like this:

Wake up anytime around ten in the morning to music being blasted in the café.

Eat a breakfast of oats, fruit, and juice while entertaining other tourists by imitating my father's Brooklyn accent.

Visit the market for precisely an hour to stare at everything but never actually buy anything.

Take my daily salsa class, eat tostadas, and then spend the entirety of the evening alongside Earth.

He's my companion, tour guide, and entertainment all in one—lucky me. I rarely speak when I'm with him, but I always listen. Do I understand what he is saying? Honestly, no. But it gives me a reason to relax and ease into the language. At night, we grab scraps of notebook paper and chill on the roof, writing lyrics to complement each other's work. The rooftop of this hostel is basically a tent city, a concrete platform where travelers set up their ragged tents and sleep side by side.

This is where Earth has been residing for some months, rolling cigarettes and scribbling words.

This evening I'm being summoned by Earth for a night-time stroll. Ain't nothing like a night-time stroll in a city as mysterious as this. We have a subtle mission to our stroll, as I've been scolded by many Guatemalans for not yet tasting *plátanos en mole*—deliciously fried plantains in a creamy and savory chocolate sauce. Tonight will put an end to that. Supposedly, a discrete vender sets up her booth in the dark evenings, cornering an alleyway, and sells delicious morsels late into the night for drunken tourists and bored locals.

I slip out of room 216 and lock the door behind me, rolled up cash stuffed into my bra as per usual. There he is, waiting directly across the hallway, looking at me with eyes matching Antigua's mysteriousness and a charming grin which makes me question my safety. His elbows rest on the balcony behind him, as he leers at my outfit of choice.

"Woah. *Que bonita, Nena.*"

I take the flattery. Who wouldn't? We're in Latin America, and let's be honest: Latin Americans have *game*. Solid, pure, handsome, intimate, and passionate game. Game that makes a Jersey girl susceptible to such spells. If only American men can take a lesson, they would learn that you won't die by simply opening a door for a woman or letting her enter a building before you. But I don't have time for American men, and they don't have time for me. I walk over, give him a big squeeze, and lock my elbow with his and together we stroll into the shadowy night.

The cobblestone streets lead us through our own fairytale that unfolds with each step. My head rests on his firm shoulders and his arm is around my waist. The nightlife booms and echoes in the city around us, but we want nothing to do with it. We're in our own bubble, inside the city, inside our minds. Tonight there happens to be a procession in which many people have traveled from all over Guatemala to attend. We do all we can to purposefully avoid it and make our way down the darkened alleyway and up to the *plátanos* vender.

I receive my plantains covered in chocolate sauce, and to be honest it would look like a smoldering pile of shit except that she sprinkled a few morsels of powdered sugar on top. Oh, Guatemala. I take my first bite as the others stand, watching me in anticipation, making me feel a new level of discomfort. I mash the already mashed plantains in my mouth, the sauce sticking to my palate. I swallow hard and look up at them, raising my eyebrow and giving a nod of acceptance. The vendor is thrilled enough to sit back down and return to her business.

Earth and I continue on our merry way, but it takes me a few paces to realize this Jester is anything but. He walks alongside me, but his head is down—real low, as if he's staring straight at his own shadow created from the fluorescent lamps overhead. His dreadlocks even look less amused. But what speaks loudest about his sudden change of mood is his silence. For the first time since I met him, a noise is not being created from the depths of his vocal cords.

Here comes the awkward part. What do I say? The little I know of Spanish is basically to communicate that I'm hungry, I want to eat, or the ingredients I'm willing to eat. I hang tight in the silence, watching our feet kiss the ground. What is the Princess supposed to do when her entertainment is down?

Be creative, I guess.

I grab his hand and start running. I'm giving him no options. He comes up alongside me and quickly sweeps ahead. Our four feet create a pounding rhythm that runs with us, all the way until we reach my destination in mind.

My favorite location in the entire city.

The water fountain.

The breasts.

I bring him straight to the edge, eye to eye with their nipples. I say absolutely nothing, letting the fountain convey it's message. I want him to see for himself the magic that I see. I want him to see the pure bounty of womanhood—the abundance, the decadence, and the pleasure. The intuition, the nourishment, and the thrill—the ladies of the fountain say it all. Seeing them in a constant state of liberation, cupping the crevices of their breasts, they are experiencing what most women don't, but what all women should: liberation and pleasure.

I come close to him, closer than I have ever come before. Sliding my body alongside his like a snake that wants to bite, but not to harm. I place my face in between his neck and shoulder, breathing him in, breathing him out. My hand meets his other cheek. I caress his soft skin with seduction, communicating through my hormones all the sensuous and delightful things that spirit intended for women to have.

I watch him melt.

But not in the way I was hoping.

Not the way I had in mind.

He takes a seat along the fountain's edge, with his elbows resting on his knees and his eyes contacting the ground. I sit beside him, shattered, transforming from the seductive Lilith to the nurturing Eve. My arm wraps around his body and I give him what all men need but don't know how to ask for: companionship and comfort.

Looking up at me, his voice breaks the silence and takes on a tone I haven't heard before: a heavy one.

"*Nena. La vida es una puta. Sabes algo, quiero decirte muchas cosas de mi vida.*"[22]

My face goes blank. He lost me already. I smile an uncertain grin. He knows this look very well. It's the face I make when I'm in need of repetition or explanation. But this time when he speaks, it's in English.

"I want to," he struggles. "I want...to tell you."

I listen like a lamb.

"I want to tell you my life, *Nena.*"

Where did he learn this English from?

I'm totally shocked.

I turn my entire body toward him, foot resting on the ledge now. I'm in full attention, summoned and bewitched like I've never been before. I keep my mouth closed, not wanting even the faintest of noises to massacre this moment.

"My life, Nena…. My life is...crazy."

He tries hard to find the next words.

"My life. When I am small boy. Is very sad."

He pauses again and looks my way.

"My life is very sad."

There he is, the Jester, but this time around he wears a frown. How hadn't I known? It all makes sense now. The questionable danger of his smile, the mysteriousness of his eyes, the indescribable desire to make others laugh—it all comes from his own pain, the pain in which he hides underground, under his surface. This is the story of the Jester, the front man, the clown. Jesters are magicians, pulling humor from life's atrocities to delight and please. They're like the

---

22 Life is a bitch. You know something? I want to tell you many things about my life.

mycelium of a forest, decomposing debris of the human heart and soul to transform it into potential joy.

Anyone who knows a Jester knows this: glory does not come without grief. For one to access such an important role, they must go through an initiation journey. This is when life chooses to deliver the most misfortunate scenarios to the Jester in training: hardships, heartbreak, and horrors. To graduate from this initiation, the Jester must bear the weight of burden all while keeping an element of enthusiasm.

The Jester's motto is "the show must go on," and thus the show will. It's only when the Jester walks backstage and removes his silly little hat in front of that mirror, he sees the permanent scars upon his face. This is when he remembers where he truly comes from. The Jester is in a constant state of being tested, being initiated, and being trained.

I suddenly see now what I hadn't been able to before: the missing parts of his story and the deeper reason behind his actions. The Jester is much more than giggles and glee. The Jester is suffering, trauma, and tragedy. Already aware he has grown up in the ghetto, I'm terrified to know what exactly this young man lived through, yet the woman inside me yearns to know. I'm ashamed to say that I haven't given much thought to his background and who he actually is as a person up until now.

But isn't this always the case?

I stay silent for a bit longer before asking a question which reaches down deeper.

"How? ¿Como?"

He proceeds carefully, rummaging through his mind to find the words he believes would communicate the best.

"Difficult. My life. Always difficult...Mi papa...es dead."

His words come out vulnerable and defeated.

I take my hand away from his shoulder, not knowing if I am helping or hurting.

But isn't this always the case?

"Nena. When mi papa die, I am very sad boy."

He glances down now, the once invisible shadow now clearly showing itself.

"My life is very sad, Nena."

Being a woman, my heart simply and naturally breaks.

I don't ask for the details.

I don't ask for more.

I hear only what is shared and offer only what I can: myself.

He stands up and shakes off his own words like someone who has witnessed a crime they wish they hadn't. I drop it. It's not my place to dig further, though I was just about to show up with the shovel. In the royal distance, a large bell sounds, alerting us of the hour. It's midnight, perfect timing, because our mission must continue.

"*Vamos.*"

The Jester walks forward and the Princess skips to follow. He leads me right out of the park, away from my safe little fountain and up to a brightly lit storefront. He asks me for twenty centavos. I consider it a donation. He makes his purchase and hands me one out of the two cigarettes.

"*Vamos.*"

I don't smoke.

He does.

So why two cigarettes?

We arrive at an alleyway leading us to a gated area. The gate is open. We slip through. We walk around the back end of a building. No one is in sight. We approach a shallow cave made of rocks. I stop dead in my tracks as he enters.

What's inside of that cave is looking at me just as much as I am looking at it.

Or rather, *him.*

He's only made of wood, but he looks as if he's alive, alive with mischief, alive with obscenity. Seated on a wooden chair, he's dressed in a red Guatemalan fabric with a bandana tied around this carved wooden throat. He wears a straw hat atop his head, to cover up the bald spots, I suppose. Around him are dried flowers, tarnished bowls of burnt frankincense, and cigarette butts, simply scattered everywhere.

Candles flicker as Earth bends down to light his cigarette with the flame. He looks toward me with a face on the verge of revenge, and his eyes say it all. "This is the hidden side of me. Take it or leave it." He brings the cigarette to his lips in a cinematic motion, all the while never taking his eyes off mine. It feels like a threat, to have these two occult men staring directly at me.

Earth summons me closer with one word.

"*Venga.*"

I oblige and step forward exactly five paces, taking my place alongside him.

"*¿El cigarrillo?*" He holds out his hand.

I take the cigarette out of my pocket, seemingly willing to do anything he tells me at this point. He lights it with his cigarette and hands it back to me.

"*En la boca,*" and as he says this his eyes lift, gesturing toward the withered face of the seated figure. [23]

Like a Guatemala version of "pin the tail on the donkey," I know exactly where I need to go. The cigarette hadn't been for me, foolish though I was. I step forward with pure

---

23   In the mouth.

hesitance and place the lit cigarette inside the carved mouth of the saint.

As I step back, I faintly hear the deep, wrinkled voice of an old man thanking me, an old man who has lived for far too long alongside far too many vices. But the vices are his friends, and they keep him tethered to Earth. The vices are the only reason he's alive and thriving. The vices give meaning to his life.

Earth takes a long and lasting drag on his dwindling smoke, then bends down and twists it on the concrete ground, releasing it from his fingertips and leaving it exactly where it has fallen.

"*Vamos.*"

THE TUNNEL OF LIFE, DEATH, AND PRAYERS

———

We enter the elongated tunnel.

I can hardly see his features through the shadows, but I know he's watching me.

"Shh," he hisses. "*Respecto, Nena.*"

Darkness closes in, welcoming us underground.

In his hands, he holds a few necessary items: burning candles and cigarettes. As he tiptoes ahead, I tiptoe behind, not taking my vision away from the flickering light. The damp walls of the tunnel press up against my arm, moistening my skin like a wet kiss. Our feet connect with the gravel below, creating the soundtrack to this moment. We're surrounded by cave walls. We're entirely alone.

The obscurity of the cave triggers the recent memory of Antigua—so close yet so far away. I'm reflecting on the night our fate was sealed, when the clock tower struck midnight and I placed that lit cigarette into the mouth of ol' Maximón. It was a night where vices had paved the road of good intentions. I sealed that night with a little more than a kiss as we locked ourselves in a union, creating our own vice.

Before we left Antigua, I made the most important purchase of my life, so now the old saint is always with us, protecting us as we dabble with danger. The miniature figurine sits snuggly in my backpack while in transit. The moment we arrive to a new location, we tend to Maximón and his ample needs, propping him up on a windowsill, chair, or desk, lighting candles and laying little candies down at his feet.

I watch Earth lead the way in the tunnel, chanting to himself in a low voice. The flame bounces, wiggles, and dances, but does not go out. I observe it, mesmerized, zoned in, and suddenly my mind is transported to Guatemala City...

Earth's stomping grounds:

The reason for arrival is none other than a rap battle, a real-life Guatemalan rap battle, and a large one. Earth isn't a participant, but a judge, which makes me feel like a Princess even more, having access to the front row and all. Or, more accurately, a seat on the concrete park floor alongside him. The musicians arrive on the scene all sorts of messed up, and I observe each one dutifully from behind my veil. I watch the way they grab at their baggy pants, raise containers of alcohol to the sides of their mouths, and spit wads of mucus in between the shoes of their opponents.

Don't fret, I'm not that judgmental. It's just a different crew than I'm used to. The tattoos, the piercings, the hair colors, the clothing—it doesn't mean they aren't respectful. It doesn't mean they aren't human. Sure, I'll admit they frighten me. They aren't easy on the nervous system, but their characters are real, and we all know by this point that I like characters. But maybe it's truly for the better I won't understand their lyrics tonight.

I take a seat as the battle begins. Immediately, like raging dogs, they go after each other. I imagine if they were dogs, they would go directly for the throat. The jugular in particular. The duality of this scene is endearing though, for no matter the snarl on their face and the intensity of their words, they are all brothers, friends, and homies. This is just a part of how they release the tensions of life in the ghetto, for they carry with them a silent mutual understanding and respect.

I munch on a bag of *Tortrix* chips and enjoy the entertainment before me, using my linen scarf to fan away the thick fumes of cigarette smoke.

Are they talented?

I'd say so, but not with a capital T.

Two hours later the winner is officially crowned for having the most creative and heart-sabotaging lyrics. Everyone plays fair around here, so they shake sweaty palms, accept their fate, and scatter back into the streets from which they came—us, too. I'm semi-stoned from the secondhand smoke, viciously hungry, and devoutly curious as to where we're heading next. I follow behind Earth like a loyal dog as he drags me out of the park, into a taxi van, and to his friend's house right in the heart of the pristine ghetto.

The first thing I notice are the Christmas lights, sloppily strung around the central platform of the neighborhood. A high-pitched "Jingle Bells" song plays while the cheap lights flash in different colors. It's October, which tells me these Christmas lights aren't for festivities. Meek housing structures are stacked one on top of each other. From their windows, I can see silhouettes of the ghetto life: babies, children, and mothers dining, cleaning, and communing.

Clueless to the shadows and bloodshed that haunt the streets around me, I make myself comfortable at the kitchen table and watch the "afterparty" gather around. These young men are close, tight like a pack of wolves. It never occurs to me to question my safety, not even once. I'm just too enamored by what I stand witness to. Six neighborhood friends from birth, friends who have survived the trials and tribulations of the ghetto life and who are lucky to still be alive. We're all gathered around the table. I'm the only female, the only outsider.

I watch as they break bread with smiles.

I watch as they fill each other's cup before their own.

I watch as they place loving hands on their friend's shoulder.

I watch them enjoy human relations as Earth's words pass through my mind.

"Where I come from, three dead a night is good news."

This is a behind-the-scenes experience, and I'm lucky to see it. It brings me back to the foundation of why we're all here on this interesting little planet: relationships. They're the building blocks for a decent human life. They make or break us. They protect us and ail us. What I can see in the relaxed expressions of these young men is an oath that "we're family." This raw humanity, it does something to me. I'm exposed, laid bare to my own inner judgments that I've created about other humans, humans I don't even know.

I've judged them before getting to know them, their stories, or their struggles.

I've judged them from the foundation of my own ignorance.

What type of person does that make me?

"*Nena.*"

I snap out of my mind and see him sitting there with a smile.

"*¿Que?*"[24]

"*¿Todo bien?*"[25]

"*Si mi amor. Todo bien.*"[26]

I take Earth's hand under the table and receive his kiss on the cheek.

"*Nena. ¿Estas bien?*"[27]

I snap my mind out of the memory and see Earth standing in the cave with the candle.

"*Si. Estoy bien.*"[28]

"*Vamos. Estamos cerca.*"[29]

I place my hand on the cave wall, attempting to read the rock as if it were brail. The only read I get is that this terrain is rough, uneven, and unpredictable.

"*Nena, mira,*" Earth calls out from up ahead. [30]

The dim lighting of his candle continues bouncing in the distance, beckoning me to come closer. I arrive alongside him. He points my distracted gaze toward an altar.

The altar.

The saint.

"Woah."

"*Llegamos, Nena.*"[31]

---

24 What?

25 Everything okay?

26 Yes, my love. Everything is okay.

27 Babe, are you good?

28 Yes, I'm good.

29 Let's go. We're close.

30 Baby, look.

31 We've arrived.

He wastes no time. Out of his backpack come flowers, the candle, and the two cigarettes. I take my royal position watching him, sucking in my last dose of fresh air.

"*Maximón. Estamos aquí.*"[32]

The candle flickers wildly as he places it on the uneven ground. I'm drawn to it like the temptation for something I'm not yet aware of.

"*¿Puedas ver, Nena?*"[33]

His voice hums toward me through the silent darkness. "*¿Como mi vida es loca?*"[34]

My mind glazes over, transporting me once again.

This time we are in the city of Xela.

I am sitting on the bed. He is standing up.

The hostel room is dark, except of course for two small candles aflame. I hold onto my phone. We refer to our relationship as *amor de los tres:* me, him, and the translator.[35] This is the pathetic way I've been learning more about Earth, his stories, and his initiation of Jester-hood. Right now, it's the only way and maybe the best way because it puts a good pace on all the information coming in.

All the horror.

All the hardships.

All the heartbreak.

I read his stories on my phone's screen, deleting them when I'm through, backspacing them when the story is absorbed inside of me. Feeling like a grandmother who

---

32 We are here.

33 Can you see babe?

34 How my life is crazy?

35 Love of three.

collects wise tales of all realms, I lock his stories inside my mind and place the key within my heart.

"*Cada noche, Nena. Cada noche. Mis padres estaban enamorados. Dame el teléfono.*"[36]

He grabs my phone and proceeds to type, cigarette hanging out the side of his mouth. An eerie shadow is cast across his face from the illumination of the phone. His dreadlocks amplify, looking like the legs of a hundred tarantulas. His fingers move fast and without hesitation. He hands the phone back over to me. I read meticulously, downloading the words into my hard drive.

"Every night my parents went for walks in our neighborhood, every single night. They would buy snacks, ice cream, and soda. I saw them always holding hands. My mom was in love with my dad, and he loved her, too. He treated my mother very good. This was the relationship I grew up watching. This is where I first discovered that love exists."

I look up at him.

"*¿Y que paso?*"[37]

He grabs the phone and takes his time to write out the continuation of his story. My eyes grace the ground as he does, imagining what could've possibly occurred. My imagination does not match what I read.

"Their oldest son, my brother, was killed. Shot three times in the back while at his friend's wedding. This was when my life became horrible. Everything changed for me. My father started drinking. A lot. He became an alcoholic and left the family. My mother became angry and took it out on me and my siblings. I had no choice but to become the adult of the

---

36 Every night baby, every night. My parents were in love. Give me the phone.

37 And what happened?

house at age eleven. I looked after my younger siblings. I protected my sister from my mother's beatings. I found a way to make money and survive."

My hands begin to tremble. He takes a puff of the cigarette, awaiting my reply. I manage to type into the translator, "How did you do it?"

He reads my message. A sarcastic chuckle leaves his mouth. Taking a final drag of the cigarette, he puts it out on the windowsill and takes a seat across the room. Typing his story, he gives away all the details. I wait with my legs crossed on the edge of the bed, never taking my eyes off him.

He walks toward me and hands over the phone, standing directly over me. Now it's his turn to keep his eyes fixated, casting his shadow over me.

"Many, many things. Things I don't want to talk about, but since you ask, I'll tell. I know you can handle it, baby. Around that age I got invited to attend a meeting. I knew a little about the reason for the meeting, but not the full details. My closest friends told me not to go. I was in so much emotional pain, I felt I had no choice but to show my face. I went to that meeting and I listened to their mission. They were going after two guys in the neighborhood who had done them wrong. They needed someone to take care of them."

Sensing in my body where this story is about to go, I force myself to remove my eyes from the screen, bringing them up to meet his in an attempt to preserve the last molecule of innocence I see in him.

"I volunteered for the mission. I did it. I did it so well that they put me in charge. I planned the extortions. I managed the team. I made the money. I used the cash to buy my mother a new home, in the ghetto of course. I used it to buy myself and my siblings new shoes. Sometimes I would give the money back to beggars and the homeless. But mostly I used it to save my family, to feed them."

My hand comes to my chin as I scroll down.

"Life has its hardships, baby, and there was one thing I couldn't save. That was the death of my father. While I was occupied with the brotherhood, my father's health went downhill rapidly and without warning. When I visited him on his deathbed, the last thing he said to me was, 'You'll be following right behind me unless you change your son of a bitch ways.' That is how I said goodbye to my father."

I look up at him, my brain split in half. I look at his hands, the ones that shed blood. I look into his eyes, the ones that have seen bloodshed. All I want to do is run for my dear fucking life, run far, far away from him. But I see his expression change upon watching the horror in my face, and a translator is not needed for what it tells me.

"I regret the things I've done. I regret them so much. Please don't judge me. I already have that taken care of."

"*¿Cuantas personas?*"[38]

I ask because I want to know.

I want to know how many people have fallen under his actions.

He takes a step back, allowing me to see his entire body through the obscure candlelight. He brings his gaze down, then shifts it upward locking eyes directly with me. He raises his right hand slowly, answering my question. My focus shifts to his pointer finger, middle finger, ring finger, and pinky.

I have two choices.

1. To run in judgment.
2. To step closer in forgiveness.

---

38 How many people?

You know me well enough by now, don't you?

It would be too easy to judge. It would be too easy to run. I step forward and take him into my arms, knowing he is ashamed, knowing of his regrets. For the first time since his father passed, I hold him and let him break down. The trauma, the wounds, and the abandonment as a child all combined with his unfortunate life scenario. He's made poor decisions, but did he have a choice? At first, no. But when the option finally came around, he took it. He left the city to flee from his past, to redeem his mistakes, to be the Jester in service of other's pain.

He hides his tears, but I feel them against my skin, damp and stagnant, jailed for all these years but relieved to finally be set free.

Like the women of the water fountain, the flowing tears bring on liberation.

"*Nena,*" he calls out to me from the depths of the cave.

"*¿Nena, sabes algo? Tengo el nombre de mi padre.*"[39]

I shake my head fast, pushing away the startling memory. Woah. How far did I just go there?

"*¿Que?*"

"*Tenemos el mismo nombre. Yo y mi padre.*"[40]

His cigarette is already halfway burnt.

He lights a second one and does his good deed of placing it into the mouth of Maximón.

And yes, all Maximón altars have a hole for this particular reason.

A hole that will never be filled.

It's inevitable.

---

39 Do you know something babe? I have the name of my father.

40 We have the same name, my father and I.

***

Who knew a Jester has so much to teach the Princess?

It makes sense, though. The Princess is as sheltered as they come. She is confined to the castle walls where she's put into a constant state of training to someday take her mother's position. King and Queen of the household may think this the best option for their precious peach, but as I'm learning through interacting with Earth, this is the most dangerous lifestyle for women.

You know why?

Because it keeps a woman naive.

Naivety is a trophy that is better when not rewarded. A naive woman can never change the world. A sheltered woman will never be tested to trust her intuition. A veiled woman will not learn how to interact with her community just outside the kingdom. And tell me, when a woman lacks all of these qualities, how is she ever to become a Queen, not just to her household, but to the whole world?

I accept my humble role as a Princess, I do.

But it never occurred to me that I'm a Princess.

Not until I locked eyes with the Jester.

I'd been unaware.

I'd been naive.

The Jester is the one that the Princess runs to when she's in need of comic relief, or when she needs to break away from the tight grip of her upbringing.

The Jester is to be trusted with a special task. If the Princess happens to ask the Jester to be escorted outside of the castle walls, behind her parents' backs, he will meet her at the edge of the forest and voyage alongside her throughout the wild terrain. The Jester will show her just what she's been missing, what's been hidden from her, what she's been ignorant of. Journeying with the Jester and listening to his life experiences is the most vital initiation for the Princess to transform into a Queen.

She just needs to trust him.

A lot.

Like, with her dear life.

So that one day she can trust herself.

And when the Jester exposes her to truths that break her little naive heart, then the Jester will take care of things by saying.

"It is life, *Nena*. It is life."

Don't be fooled now.

The Princess isn't the only one who gains highly from this experience.

It's certainly a two-way street.

When the Jester accepts his humble place of enlightening the Princess, he's also saying yes to being taught by her fluid and feminine ways. He will teach her to be of the world and she will teach him how to be in the world. In a state of gratitude, her soft and innocent hands will grace his cheeks, her gentle lips will find his, and in this intimate encounter the Jester will remember that love certainly does exist.

The Jester may do whatever he wishes with the golden kiss of love that the Princess gifts him. It's a token of gratitude he may keep, even when the Princess leaves him behind. He's earned it for all his loyal efforts. He may decide to store it in his back pocket like a sacred keepsake, only to be remembered during daunting times. Or, in some rare cases, the Jester may realize his true potential with that golden kiss, and in doing so he can use it to finally retire his position as Jester and transform himself into King.

A group of locals enters the cave. Draped in colorful Guatemala fabric, they shuffle past us in the dim tunnel while chanting in their native tongue: Quiché. Their candles flicker through the clouds of smoke surrounding Maximón and his altar. They pay no attention to us. They allow us to be.

Earth turns to me, his dreadlocks creating an obscure shadow.

His face is barely visible behind the lingering haze of his cigarette and the heaviness of his history.

He whispers to me.

"Deanna..."

"¿Sí?"

"*Gracias por todo.*"[41]

My heart melts.

"*Gracias a ti también.*"[42]

I smile at the simple understanding of why we meet the people we do, when we do.

When the Princess is ready for transformation, the Jester holds the candle and guides the way.

All she needs to do is trust him.

We walk out of the tunnel, hand in hand, guided together by the light at the opening.

---

41   Thank you for everything.

42   Thank you too.

THE THIN WHITE
LINE OF PARANOIA

———

We stand on the side of the road, halfway to Mexico with our two thumbs sticking out happy-go-lucky.

The sun is not a hitchhiker's best friend, and neither is the rain. But a hitchhiker takes whatever they are given, usually. There's a lesson of patience and trust to be learned while hitchhiking. You cannot force people to stop; you must wait for them to make the decision, putting your adventure into their hands. Trust me when I say you really don't want just *anyone* to stop. While hitchhiking you better have damn good intuition, an army of angels, or both, before you get into someone's closed, moving vehicle. Someone who is going your direction with good intentions is the best-case scenario, and the only scenario you should pray for while hitchhiking in Central America.

Luck is on our side today, as we've already scored three wonderful rides and have traveled over two hundred miles with a brother and sister in a Honda Civic, an employee in a semi-trailer with snacks and good music, and an adorable family with three curious-eyed children. We are nearing the border where Guatemala ends and Chiapas begins. Our plan is to make it to San Cristobal by this evening to celebrate New Year's weekend in the mighty city.

Up in the distance a sleek black car begins to slow down. This is the cue every hitchhiker looks for: the slowdown. It's a slice of heaven served with hope.

The car eases off the road and rolls right up to us. As the tinted window comes down, I see the face of a young man in the passenger seat and a middle-aged man in the driver's seat.

"Hello. Where are you going?"

His accent is present, but his English is clear. I walk up to the car to speak for us, and as I bring my body closer to the vehicle I notice two young men in the backseat dressed in sleek attire, with thick dark hair styled to perfection. Their watches wink at me.

"We're heading toward the border."

"Get in."

Sometimes intuition isn't always correct.

And sometimes it isn't even present.

I look toward Earth who stands confused, not with the dialogue, but at the fact we're entering the vehicle. We squeeze in, me in the middle and him on the end. He closes the door with a hard slam and the car rolls forward.

We're in motion.

"So, do you like Guatemala?" the driver asks, peeking at me from his rearview mirror, trimmed mustache covering his upper lip.

"I had no choice but to come back here."

"Oh, this is your second time here?"

"Well, not really. I was supposed to fly to Colombia, but I missed my flight and decided to stay so I can spend more time with this one." I point my thumb to my right.

"Oh, where is he from?"

"From here. *Guate.*"

"So you've fallen in love with a Guatemalan?"

I look over toward Earth, whose hands are grasped together and resting atop his backpack. His eyes are glazed over, attempting to make sense of the conversation. The young men aside me remain silent, looking off into the distance.

"Something like that."

"And why are you going to Mexico?" He peeks his head again in the rearview mirror, looking for an expression on my face.

"For New Year's."

"How long have you been here in Guatemala?"

"A few months, more or less."

"I see. I see."

I reach for Earth's hand. It's sweaty and stiff. He doesn't look at me or mutter a single word, not until we are safely out of the car an hour later and standing back on the road. He begins to shift uncomfortably from side to side, glancing over his shoulders with fast moving eyes.

"*Dame el teléfono.*"[43]

He takes my phone in his hand and types a quick sentence, without looking at me he hands it over.

"What did they say?" The message reads.

"Nothing important. Small talk," I type back.

He rolls his eyes and types out another question.

---

43 Give me the phone.

"Did they ask about me?"

I look up at him with squinted eyes and sarcastic brows, refusing to type out this response.

"No..."

This is enough to send him rumbling like a loaded earthquake, hot and heavy in his stance, protective like a guard dog, raising his voice about the dangers of Guatemala and my naive actions. I watch as his eyes move even more rapidly all around me as he speaks. I'm oblivious to the thoughts in his mind, insensitive and ignorant at best. His rapid heart nearly vibrates the ground beneath us, which amplifies my own electrical impulses, communicating for me to remain silent and let it pass.

And pass it does.

His face breaks with a sarcastic smile and his words settle the tension. *"Esta bien, Nena. Esta bien."* [44]

We are in desolate terrain now, waiting a long while before any car passes us by. Cars are infrequent and we have a long way to go. That's the name of the game when luck runs out. The dry wind whips past our ears, creating a tunneling sounds that reminds me of where we are. The next gush of wind comes right behind the first, strong and steady, bringing with it a whimpering voice.

A voice that sounds all too familiar.

A voice that wants to speak to me.

The sun must've gotten the best of me, or maybe the car fumes.

But without warning, I hear the voice again, louder this time and clearer than before.

It's within and without, speaking with me and to me.

---

44 It's fine babe, it's fine.

Is it the voice of a man or woman?

It speaks again and I realize that it's both.

Is it my voice, or the voice of another?

It speaks again and I realize that it's both.

Is the voice speaking in Spanish or English?

It speaks again and I realize that it's both.

For a moment, the voice stops.

From behind me I feel a firm hand press down on my shoulder.

I turn around to meet his eyes.

They are red, with the pain of a wounded panther.

His face is contorted in pain.

The pain of danger.

The pain of betrayal.

The pain of paranoia.

A masculine voice speaks.

"Deanna, *necesitas cuidate!*" the outside voice expresses.[45]

A feminine voice speaks.

"Deanna, you need to watch out for yourself!" the inside voice expresses.

That's when I realize that, for different reasons, we're both afraid.

∗∗∗

I stare at the ATM machine as if it owes me something, because it does.

Inside the allotted slot my only debit card went, and like a broken boomerang it did not return. I press every button available to me, and to my horror the card is gone—lost in

---

45   You need to watch out for yourself!

transaction. I count the pesos I received earlier at the border—twenty. We need one hundred twenty to catch a minibus to San Cristobal.

I spin on my heels and look at Earth.

"¿Que paso, Nena?"[46]

"Pues...no tenemos dinero."[47]

"¿Enserio?"[48]

"Si, mira."[49]

Committed to solving the issue, he stands up and brings himself to face the ATM machine. He does nothing other than stare at it for forty-five seconds before breaking into a solid laughter. Right, that makes sense. He's never used an ATM machine in his life, so he's truly of no use. There goes my only debit card, and along with it our only means to cash. If you think Earth has money, think again. He spent it all in the previous town on my dinner and dessert. I truly am a *gordita,* regretting having eaten all those *pupusas.*[50] Since we've been traveling outside of Antigua, there hasn't been any solid bus routes Earth can perform on. No bus routes means no *centavos.* No *centavos* means I'm the provider.

Bienvenido a Mexico.

Apparently Earth is fine with the situation; it's not his first time on the streets without cash.

This is a time for me to be creative because Princess doesn't sleep on the streets, not tonight.

---

46 What happened?

47 Well, we don't have money.

48 Seriously?

49 Yes, look.

50 Flatbread cooked with corn or rice flour, cheese, and meats.

I take a seat on my backpack underneath the fluorescent lights of the small lobby. Earth is leaning up against the wall, watching me close my eyes and talk to myself like a lunatic.

"C'mon spirit, what's going on here."

There has to be another way. I refuse to believe we're stuck.

"If I can just get a little assistance, that could be nice."

I'm not in this alone. I have my meditations, of course, I do. Three years of clairvoyant training hasn't been for nothing. I do as I've been taught, rooting down and bringing myself back into my body. My mind goes clear as I deepen my breath and allow energy to flow through me. I visualize a rose, a single golden rose, a golden prayer asking for help. I watch its image and the energy surrounding it waver in and out before it disappears seemingly out of thin air.

Let's backtrack a moment.

Maybe you find this very bizarre, that I'm out of money in a town where I don't know a single soul. Night-time has fallen upon me and I have absolutely nowhere to go and no means of getting there. But what do I decide to do? Sit on my backpack and meditate?

Strange, right?

Well, let me tell you, I've seen stranger things.

And one of them has to do with being handed one hundred twenty pesos exactly when I need them.

"*Señora. ¿Estas bien?*"

A middle-aged woman crouches down to see me at eye level. I point to the ATM machine and explain the scenario. Without hesitation she pulls a few bills from her wallet, gesturing that she is more than happy to help me in any way she can. She welcomes us to Mexico and wishes us the best of luck.

The *best* of luck.

Now it's my turn to say it.

"*Vamos, mi amor.*"[51]

Earth pushes himself off the wall, cool as a cat, and follows behind me as if nothing happened.

***

The streets are dark yet decorated with a soft glow. High heels, threaded skirts, leather bags, and cowboy boots pace through the historical streets of San Cristobal. Music of many genres blare from every angle. Firecrackers pop and crackle in the distance. Stray dogs run about, fleeing the scene while searching for food. Street performers step forward to do their deeds and earn their quick cash. Humans interact in many ways, delight in their eyes and celebration in their hearts. Lovers, parents and children are all here tonight, bringing in the New Year alongside strangers alike.

Strangers like us.

At this point we're getting by on the generosity of people and pure luck alone. A few nights ago, we handed our miracle *pesos* to a bull-framed man with a handlebar mustache. He took the hard cash without smiling and stuffed our backpacks into the trunk. Behind the driver's wheel he stationed himself as all his passengers found their place behind him. The doors to the minibus closed and our fate continued.

We were dumped onto the streets of San Cristobal at midnight, give or take, and an Argentinean acquaintance became our next hero.

"Come here. We'll host you until Monday."

---

51   Let's go, my love.

He gave us the address to his friend's marbled bed and breakfast, a fantastic place for a Princess to spend the night. I marveled at my clean white sheets and royal purple comforter, consuming the entire bed just for good humor. Now tonight brings us to our ultimate night in this kingdom as we plan on returning to the town from which we came, on a mission to retrieve my debit card.

Earth and I roam the packed streets like two lost dogs who don't know that they're lost, happy and ignorant we are with what we have. As others consume hot cocoa, churros, and tamales, we walk past their shadows, observing their delight.

"*Nena. Teléfono.*"

I reach into my pocket and pass it over to him as we stroll forward without an agenda. His fingers pound the device, transporting his thoughts. He hands the phone over.

"You know something, baby? Creativity comes when we have no choice but to change our lives. If we're constantly comfortable, there will be no desire to change. Creativity is a part of evolution. It's what makes life fun."

I read his words over and over, making sense of his belief.

"What makes you say this?" I type back.

He reads the message and halts dead in his tracks, typing furiously. Impatiently awaiting his response, I find myself drifting over to a painted mural down the street. The mural greets me, beckoning me to come closer, to be with its message. I look up to see the face of a local elderly woman painted to perfection. Her wrinkles tell a tale of time while her eyes tell a tale of pain. She sheds teardrops which flow into a river below. Spelled out beneath her is written, "*Lo Único Que Tenemos Es Amor.*"

"The only thing we have is love."

"*Nena, aquí.*" We switch places now, my eyes on the phone and his on the mural, and here we stand, back-to-back, for a solid minute, me looking down and him looking up. He reads the message behind the image as I read the message behind his words.

"I believe that traveling is a form of creativity and I say this for many reasons. I see it all the time with *gringos.* You come to our countries with your money and you choose to have whatever experience you wish. You can all buy your way through it. I see how most tourists follow the crowd; they do what they're told. Is that traveling? Tell me. They're too comfortable to care, and very few will step out of this comfort zone."

I scroll down to reveal more of his novel.

"When the *gringos* come down and stay in their fancy hostels within their comfort zones, they have no desire to experience our culture in its deepest roots or expose themselves to the wisdom that the land has to offer. They are shrinking their creativity instead of expanding it. That's not traveling to me. Traveling to me is allowing yourself to have nothing so you can experience anything. This opens you up to thinking for yourself, to creating relationships and lasting connections and to get yourself out there in the world. In doing so you meet people who educate you, teach you, and adore you. It's a test and a quest all in one."

His words hit me deep in my core. He's right. I think back to the land from which I come. How many people sit comfortably atop of their riches? How many people who are seated atop these riches ever feel motivated enough or creative enough to even think about making a change? Comfort is a breeding ground for ignorance. I'm not necessarily referring to physical resources. Mostly it stems from the mind and what people decide to accept as their reality, or not. We all have the ability to create and some of us just choose to access it in different ways.

I screenshot his beautiful message and type my own.

"Your words are strong, my love, and certainly I'm learning a lot from you. As you know I'm a *gringa,* but I hope you have seen me in a unique light. I hope you see in me a willingness to understand and learn.[52] To be honest, it actually feels good to not have money these past few days as it's been teaching me about where my distractions lie, and the spaces I use to escape. It goes deeper than I know. What I've been noticing is that my mind is more present. I'm truly here to experience the only thing we have: love."

I spin around to hand him the phone, watching as the bright screen lights up his face, my words igniting his smile. He lingers in this space for a moment, and before I can blink the phone is shut off and thrown into his pocket. His hand is behind my head, lips pressed against mine. He kisses me unrelenting, pressing my body up against the painted mural. My head hovers directly below one of the old woman's tears, as if it's entering my crown, either blessing me, or cursing me, or both.

I kiss him back with force, pulling his solid frame closer to me, my hands on his cheeks. Breathing in the scent of his story, the essence of his humanness. Under the ominous streetlamp we stand, arms entangled, and stories forever intertwined. He brings me down to his depths, the dark depths of the forest. Without the tethers of money, I feel free. Perhaps for a split second I see the faint glimpse into the richness of poverty, a notion which transcends greed and

---

52 A Caucasian, typically of North American descent.

commits one to a life of community, family, and hopefully a healthy state of mind. These, I'm learning, are the true threads of life embedded in gold, making one a rich man.

"*Por eso te amo, Nena. Por tu mente. Por tu corazón.*"[53]

He loves me?

He loves me.

For my mind and my heart.

I remain silent, kissing him back.

One doesn't need money to make love, at least not in this situation.

***

There's a man to my left. I don't know his name, yet here I sit alongside him, sandwiched in the middle between Earth and this quiet stranger. We're high up above the road, very, very high. He concentrates on driving his eighteen-wheeler down the desolate backroads of Chiapas. This is what happens when you do things that your parents don't approve of. You end up in stranger's cars. This is also what happens when you lose your only debit card. You take any ride you can get, in hopes that you can retrieve what is yours.

I plan to barge into that bank, demand my slice of plastic, and carry on with life.

We've sat silently in the truck for over twenty minutes. The driver isn't saying a word, isn't even giving us the decency of a faint smile or a simple question. With a serious face he keeps his eyes focused, hypnotizing himself by the road ahead. Out of my peripheral vision I see him fidgeting. Without taking his eyes off the road, he reaches for a compartment

---

53 This is why I love you baby, for your mind, for your heart.

underneath the dashboard and pulls out a pack of cigarettes. Marlboros. Opening up the pack with one hand, he offers them to us. Earth reaches across my chest to grab one and together they light up.

The lingering fumes of the smoke ease the tension inside of the truck—for the two guys. As for me, I'm trying to breathe what little fresh air I can.

"*¿De donde son?*" [54]

The driver glances over to get a better look at us.

"*Soy de Guatemala y ella es de los Estados Unidos.*" [55]

I remain quiet and watch the scene unfold.

"*¿Estados Unidos?*" He looks me over again.

"*Si.*"

"*Ah. Que bueno.*" The driver takes a long, exaggerated inhale on his burning cigarette before speaking again.

"*¿Son novios?*" [56]

"*Si.*" Earth flicks his ash out the window.

"*Que bueno. Ella es muy bonita.*" The driver looks me over a third time, taking his ultimate drag before tossing the cigarette out the window. [57]

I shift in my seat, uneasy under the gaze of this stranger.

The conversation ends there, and the ride continues in silence.

There's a new form of tension now, one that's palpable.

I don't turn my head. I don't even blink. The driver fixates his serious face on the road once more, but now his hand begins to search for something else. A shock ripples through

---

54 Where are you two from?

55 I'm from Guatemala and she is from United States.

56 Are you a couple?

57 That's good. She is very pretty.

me. The truck engine grows louder in my ears as my senses heighten drastically. I watch, through my peripheral once again, the movements of the man's hand. He's still moving it around, in search of whatever.

I dare not look. I dare not blink.

The two guys, one on either side of me return back to their conversation, one I no longer understand. This time they are laughing, a casual laugh, as the energy inside this truck continues to pulsate. The strange man finds what he's been looking for. A rectangular mirror. I keep my eyes stationed forward as he lines up the bleached white substance across the glistening mirror. He does it with a perfection that is slightly impressive, I must admit, as he allows it to rest on his lap for a moment. Every single gram stays in the line as he pulls over to ask a few neighborhood kids for directions.

Even if I wanted to, I cannot look.

The scene stumbles on, like the scene to a fantastic film, one that I'm a part of. Both of his hands release the steering wheel, bringing the mirror up to his nose to do the deed. Something ripples through me as if it was I who took the line. What happens next is inevitable, really. The tiny glistening mirror with half a line is passed in my direction. I don't move. I don't look at it. I don't take it. Instead a caramel arm reaches across me and grips the mirror.

The moment the mirror touches his hand, I glance down at it. My eyes not fixating on the white line, but instead I'm drawn to a fragment of my reflection, looking back at me. Earth has the mirror in his possession now.

I mechanically turn my head to the right.

I look into the eyes of the person I've been learning to trust.

"No."

My voice is a sacrifice.

"*Por favor. No.*"

I shake my head very gently from side to side in that robotic manner. These are the only two words I can muster up, though my eyes say much more. The fear they yield is enough to be considered, communicating the fear for my safety as a woman, a foreigner. Through my eyes I try to tell him of the betrayal that will organically happen if he decides to indulge.

He looks back at me while holding the mirror in his hands. His colorful dreadlocks surrounding his easeful face.

"*Eres tan linda, Nena,*" he says it with a laugh. [58]

My face flushes of all cardiovascular activity, turning me as white as the substance residing on the mirror.

My gaze automatically whips forward.

I do not look. I cannot look.

I swallow the bulging large lump of fear and betrayal and keep my eyes on the road in front of me, the road that rolls over and over. I ask it to hypnotize me so that I can enter into a calmer place, a softer place.

A place called withdrawal.

The mirror is passed back over to the driver.

Void of substance.

***

For the amount of experiences I've had in my twenties, I'll be honest in saying that mind-altering substances haven't been a part of them, except for the occasional shot of LaoLao, of course. Perhaps it's something embedded in my DNA, or

---

58   You are so cute, baby.

maybe there is a fear of the unknown with these substances, but my intentions have always been to experience life as it comes, in an organic state and with the mind I wake up with.

Thus far, it has worked well for me.

Here's how I see it, but I'm aware that my opinion falls short in the realm of other people's truth: we have a battle ahead of us, and it's a battle of consciousness. Over the years of constant wars, mind control operations, and food alteration, throughout the courses of genocides, mass murders of the indigenous, the rise of consumerism, and institutionalization, we've become no better than a dog on their leash.

They think for us, the people on top, of course, and we've been allowing them to do it for many centuries. What it has established is a disconnected population of people who've lost their highway to "source." See source as you will—intuition, God, enlightenment, the spirit. Each individuals' relationship to source combines with others in their local communities and spans out, adding to the overall tone of consciousness in this world. When people in masses alter their consciousness, they alter their reality of life on Earth. It's about coming together instead of being separated.

To change the world, consciousness must be raised. Any Fool, no matter how naive, can take a step back and see that the world is in a state of disgrace. To step forward in the battle, we must step out of a consciousness that is manipulated, suppressed, and forgotten, and transform it into a state where it's heightened, awoken, and healed. We must strengthen our connection to source through our individual bond, our communal bond, and the evolution of our consciousness will raise.

Well, how do we do that?

Do you think we can do that by staring at a TV screen?

Do you think we can do that by consuming copious amounts of alcohol?

Do you think we can do that by inhaling substances into every crevice of our bodies?

The truth of these questions lie within you, but I'll share what I've learned for myself. Evolving consciousness begins with being in our body, coming back to square one. We must inhabit the vehicle we've been gifted, calling consciousness into it instead of looking for it "out there." Any mind-altering substances are "out there," meaning you must reach outside your body to have an experience, and though they may lead you to truths, what good do these truths do if you can't have them in your body?

Or maybe you can.

So you take that line of coke.

***

Their laughter sounds like mutated voices from afar, two Jesters among a single Princess. I'm clearly the odd one out. It brings me back to my childhood being the middle child, the black sheep. I'm convinced they are laughing at me, just like my brothers once did. They're laughing at my anger and my emotions. They're taunting my inability to understand that not all want the same out of life.

One to my left and one to my right.

One older, one younger.

I'm in the middle.

I'm in the middle.

I'm in the middle.

Everything that happens in that vehicle happens directly unto me, running through me like a wave of energy and emotion, because I'm in the middle. I've always been in the middle.

He tries to get my attention.

"*Deanna.*"

"*Nena...*"

"*¿Que? ¿Estas enojada?*[59]"

"*Bien Deanna.*"

The red comes rushing on like a thousand-year-old river suddenly let loose for the first time.

The red is anger.

The river is my body.

It takes me a lifetime to realize what I am.

I am angry.

Then it takes me just a moment to set myself free because the one in the middle always has a choice.

***

The truck stops smack in the center of another dusty and deserted road. I do not look at the driver or thank him for stopping. Instead, I grab my torn backpack, crawl over Earth, and kiss my feet to the ground. Crossing the other side of the road, I walk.

Away from Earth.

The wind blows furiously, whipping a tumbleweed past me.

In seeing this, I *almost* laugh.

Then the voice returns, the same voice that comes with the wind.

Both of them.

The one in Spanish and the one in English.

---

59 Are you mad?

The masculine one and the feminine one.

I feel a hand placed on my shoulder from behind me.

I turn around and look into his eyes.

They are red, with the fear of a wounded panther, now matching that of mine.

Our faces are contorted in pain.

The pain of danger.

The pain of betrayal.

The pain of paranoia.

The voice speaks again.

"*Deanna. ¡Necesitas cuidate!*" he says to me.

"Deanna! You need to watch out!" I say to myself.

We are both paranoid of each other's wisdom.

His of the darkness. Mine of the light.

¡SON AVENTURAS!

———

I arrive mid-morning to the only building on the street that's painted in a rich azul. It's the ultimate sign telling me I've arrived. Clutching the harness of my backpack, I notice my surroundings are empty, an uncommon phenomenon for a cultural place like Mexico City. As I press my finger into the hidden doorbell, the silence is invasively shattered by a barking dog.

The door swings open with a jolt, allowing me an immediate glance toward the furry beast wagging his tail like a devil, projecting his voice toward me. I trail my gaze up, slowly, to the tall figure hovering over both the dog and myself, the owner of the radically blue house, I suspect. He is a smiling man with a philosophical appearance, a head of white hair, and a white mustache outline his age, which simultaneously lie hidden behind his youthful smile.

The dog ceases his barking to pounce on me upon entering.

"*Bienvenido,* Deanna."

Ernesto's smile becomes a source of invitation into his home. The dog aims for my face as I smile back. I follow Ernesto up a flight of twinkling marble stairs. He opens another door leading into a beautiful bedroom filled with light from the bright sun peeking just behind the windows.

"*Aquí tienes*. Rest and we'll see you for lunch." Ernesto places my bag atop the bed frame and slips out of the door from which we came.

"*Bruno! ¡Ven!*"

The dog scoots out of the room on his heels, following right behind Ernesto and leaving me in solitude.

I unpack my bag, item by item, until I'm left with an empty and lifeless backpack. I place my journal on the glass desk alongside my ukulele and the contents of my wallet, including my restored debit card. I glance past the mirror. It asks me to stop what I'm doing and look up. My face is bronzed but sticky with sweat. I run my hands through my knotted hair, combing through it. Then I see my eyes. They look as if I've just crawled out of the wilderness, deep and tired, angry yet forgiving. I shut them, and my mind takes me to his eyes.

Deep, tired, and gone.

***

"*Mucho gusto, Deanna.*"

Ernesto's wife gives me a kiss on the cheek and motions for me to take a seat in the dining room. Bruno follows her every move as she lays a warm bowl of *Pozole* in front of me.[60]

"*Provecho.*"[61]

I add avocado on top, sprinkling the bowl with salt and lime juice.

---

60 A traditional Mexican soup made of hominy, vegetables and meats.

61 Enjoy.

"*Gracias, Antonia.*"

"*De nada.*"

We eat in silence, except for Bruno's whimpers. The warm soup nourishes me, replenishing my mood and rejuvenating my body. I ended up here by chance alone. After fleeing the eighteen-wheeler and retrieving my card in Chiapas, I took a night-time bus through the southern part of Mexico where it delivered me on the side of the road in the awakening city like a futon. Along the way I reached out to a few friends who I knew have lived here, and one of them responded with her father's phone number.

I called the number, and that was the first time I heard Ernesto's voice.

I've been invited to stay at their house while I explore the city, however long that may take. *La Ciudad de Mexico* is an incredible place of historical and cultural revolution. It's home to over one hundred fifty museums, Aztec ruins, and incredible artists such as Fridha Kahlo, Diego Rivera, and Leonora Carrington. The city is densely populated and had no option but to birth a cultural scene like no other. It has markets which go on for miles, street food that would bring Anthony Bourdain back from the dead, colorful festivals, and a population of people who smile at every chance they get.

No to mention the churros.

Or the hot cacao.

Or the tamales.

"So, Deanna. *Dime.* What do your parents think of your travels?" I look up to see Ernesto finished with his plate, elbows on the table and fingers bridged.

I bow.

"They hate it and would prefer I stay blind to the world for the sake of safety."

Ernesto looks down at the table, but I can see he is hiding his laughter.

"¡*Son gringos*! That's exactly what we need, more women being sheltered."[62]

I agree.

"What made you leave?"

"I disliked New Jersey. I needed to get out."

Ernesto leans back in his seat, removing his elbows from the table and running his fingers over his white mustache. Before speaking again he clears his throat, letting the words escape like a gentle fable.

"There is more to it, Deanna. Your dislike of *Nueva Jersey* is not the reason you left. I can see that in you immediately. You are a hot-headed *jovencita*, so you refuse to see what I see.[63] But I can tell you are not a typical *gringa*. You have a curiosity about you that is undeniable, and that curiosity has led you to learn many things, has it not?"

Fixated on his face, I nod my head slowly.

"You're still young, but you must keep learning the world. That's the only way to change it. Trust me on this one, it'll be *mujeres* who change the world.[64] Do you know why they keep women so suppressed?"

"I have an idea."

Without listening to my response, he continues.

"Because of their power. Men are afraid of *mujeres*, so they keep them little."

Antonia shifts in her seat, listening but not adding to the conversation, seemingly familiar with her husband's rants.

---

62 They are gringos.

63 You are a young one.

64 Women

"*¿Tienes un novio?*"[65]

Really?

Why does it always come down to this?

If I have a *boyfriend*?

I go to answer but I'm arrested in my tracks, recalling the occurrence just a day before. My hesitance arises a curiosity within them.

"Tell us what happened. *¿Que pasó?*"

Without any filter or hesitation, I tell them everything—as much as I've told you about Earth, and maybe even a little more. I fly off the handle, get lost in the woods, and enter the darker places of my mind. They're the perfect audience, nodding their head in unison and keeping their opinions muted, for now. I tell the story of Maximón and the tunnel, of Antigua and the debit card. I even tell the story of the eighteen-wheeler and that shiny mirror.

Ernesto crosses his arms, coming to a quick conclusion with what I shared.

"*Bueno, Deanna. No tienes un novio. Tienes una aventura, si?*"[66]

The words hit me, both hard and soft, swinging a golden flag of realization over my head like victory made simple.

He wasn't my boyfriend. He was just an adventure.

How could Ernesto see this so fast? What does he know that I don't?

"Deanna, *dime*. Your other boyfriends, have they been this way as well?"

I nearly choke on my soup, pausing to bring this realization to the rest of the matter, spanning throughout my

---

65 Do you have a boyfriend?

66 Well, Deanna, you don't have a boyfriend. You have an adventure, yes?

memories to the past years of exploration, to the feelings which were undoubtedly real, but the situations which were undoubtedly unrealistic. The intensity, the spontaneity, the lack of communication for grounded and more stable things.

The immaturity of it all.

The naivety.

¡La vergüenza!

The shame.

"Well... yeah."

Ernesto claps his hands together, bringing the realization to a close.

"*¡Son aventuras! Todos!*"[67]

Great.

They were *all* adventures.

***

In the color-drenched neighborhood of Coyoacán I go for daily strolls, keeping my hands in my pockets and my gaze down. Whenever I lift my eyes they fall upon young, very attractive couples who send me into pity. I handle the shame by visiting the many museums offered. I take my sweet time in each one, questioning how the objects, paintings, and information in front of me can make me a better person.

I happen upon the temple of Teotihuacán where I try to avoid tourists, which ultimately means I'm trying to avoid myself. I stumble upon the famous National Museum of Anthropology and watch in the courtyard as two American women create a scene over a pigeon. I come across the Museum of Memory and Tolerance, where I'm informed,

---

67 They are adventures, all!

horrifically, about the mass genocides that have taken place throughout our planet. I assume I must have been absent on these days of history class, as I only recall learning about one genocide. I walk through the walls of Leon Trotsky's house where I text a photo to my brother. He replies by asking me if I've decided to become a communist.

"No, I'm just visiting a museum."

I wait in the long line outside of La Casa Azul, Frida Kahlo's old home which has been transformed into a very popular museum. Through the rooms of her house I float, surveying and observing every molecule of her intricate yet excruciatingly painful life. Frida's bold character and fearless image inspires me. Out in the courtyard of the museum I sit to watch a short film of Frida's life. As the video ends and the people around me get up to leave, I stay. After one too many rounds, I wipe the tears from my eyes and finally do walk away.

One day I happen upon a tamale festival taking place in a culture center.

"Tamales?" I think as my body is already entering through the doors.

There's a plethora of booths, each serving hundreds of tamales. There are tamales of all sauces, sizes, and servings. I've never seen anything like this because I've never been to a tamale festival in Mexico City before. *Duh.* I walk past booths serving tamales with pork, chicken and beef. There are tamales with spicy red sauce and tamales with mild green sauce. I see tamales that are sweet, filled with fruits and creams. I see chocolate tamales and Oreo-stuffed tamales, tamales with cheese and vegetables and tamales with beans and cream.

Where to start?

I choose a vegetarian tamale and find a spot to sit down and eat. I'm drooling over the plate, impatient to dig in. Before I'm able to take my first bite, a couple stops directly in front of me to comment on how delicious my tamale looks, and to ask where, just *where*, have I purchased it from?

Occasionally I visit the nearby church, always sitting by myself in an empty pew in the back. I stare ahead aimlessly while watching as a sunray gleams through a window. By the time I leave, an hour or so later, the sunlight makes its way from that window to another, slowly gracing itself upon the bald head of a man who sits in the pew directly below it. He must've planned this, for this has happened more than once.

In this old standing church, I do all my contemplation. There is endless lulling going on inside my head, untangling of thoughts which cast shadows in my mind. I think about my role as a Princess, a woman who is still yet learning, and Earth's role as a Jester, a man who is still yet learning.

Fairytales tell us about a young Princess who goes ahead and kisses a frog, in hopes that he'll turn into a fine and loving prince, a prince good enough for her. Well, in this case, the frog was a Jester. From just one kiss, the bumpy skinned frog is supposed to transform into the face of a majestic hero, one who is already on his knees with flowers, singing to his beloved a song deep from his heart. He sees his Princess as the goddess who has transformed his life, and he promises to her that he'll be a loyal and respectful man, day after day.

This fairytale is an illusion, you see. The Jester never changes under the pressure of the Princess's expectation. Any transformations perceived through the eyes of the Princess could be a devastating illusion. The "prince" she sees in him is a projected fantasy of who she wants the Jester to become alongside her. She can easily lose focus on bettering herself by putting all her focus on bettering him. This is a slippery slope, for both the Jester and the Princess can only be made "better" by having their own journeys, learning from their own mistakes, and going through their own initiation process.

Though she can offer a kiss to the Jester, the kiss lies upon his cheek, and he has a choice in what he decides to do with it.

Plain and simple.

***

I slip my body through the front door, closing it behind me as gracefully as I can so as not to wake Bruno. The night sky disappears behind the door, transporting me to a dimly lit living room.

"Deanna. Sit, please."

I nearly jump out of my skin, not having known Ernesto was still awake.

He motions his hand out in front of me, gesturing toward the rickety woven chair.

I get myself situated, and he immediately begins his discussion.

"There are three main events that take place in one's life, three monumental events. Do you know what they are?"

At this, Ernesto rests his elbows on the unstable table, bringing the tips of his fingers together, creating that bridge and resembling a philosopher. I squint my eyes as the already rampant motors in my mind runs in aims of answering his riddle. He begins to count them off before I can provide my own thoughts.

"The first is marriage when you recite the vows, making the commitment to accompany someone throughout their entire life. Understand?"

I nod my head.

"Okay, *bueno*. The second is the event of bringing children into this world, creating a home and foundation for your blood to thrive. *Si?*"

I nod my head.

"Now, can you tell me the third?"

This time I close my eyes completely, paying attention to the course of life he is taking me through. I postulate in my head what he would like me to say, but the answer simply does not appear. I open my eyes, blank and weary, asking for mercy. At my dumbfounded silence he gracefully raises his hand and points to an old photograph hanging daintily on the wall alongside us. The photograph shows an elderly couple sitting side by side.

"*Son mis padres*. They are both passed."[68]

I take a moment to absorb the photograph, black and white, tinted by the sun. The middle-aged man and woman inside of the frame smile, but only slightly, showcasing their run-ins with hardship. They hold each other's hand and stare straight ahead. I can see the resemblance to Ernesto's father, that philosophical appearance.

"Deanna, the third major event in one's life is the death of their parents."

This time I nod, but with hesitance. Having experienced none of these three major events, I'm yearning to know where this discussion will lead.

"Deanna, you haven't experienced this yet, have you?"

I shake my head no.

"If all goes well, you one day will experience this and it will be the only event out of the three that you don't have a

---

68 They're my parents.

choice in. The rest of these events you'll have a choice. You can decide if you want to get married, and to whom. You can decide to bring children into this world as well. But you cannot decide if your parents will pass, nor when. *¿Entiendes?*"[69]

I stare past his spectacles and into his deep-set eyes.

Eyes of mystery. Eyes of knowledge.

"*Si. Entiendo.*"[70]

"*Bueno.* And you have two brothers?"

I nod.

"We spoke of this earlier, but I need to explain to you further exactly what makes women more powerful than men. It's their emotions. Women have access to their emotions in ways men do not. Deanna, one day when you parents do pass, you'll have the tools to process it. *¿Por que? Porque eres una mujer.* Because you're a woman Deanna, and women have the natural ability to feel their emotions and release them. Your brothers on the other hand, one day you'll see they'll be stuck, stuck in the pain and the anger. *¡Son enojados!* They'll have a hard time. I'm telling you this because the world needs women like you who aren't afraid to explore and feel, to get hurt and learn. The world needs women who can nurture themselves while taking care of others. The world needs more women who are curious. Through this, the world evolves and we can heal and humanity move forward."[71]

I nod in shock, in delight, and in horror.

Maybe out of coincidence, or maybe not, but Ernesto has certainly hit the nail on the head. The depths of my darkness have just exposed themselves: my deepest fears come from

---

69 Do you understand?

70 Yes, I understand.

71 They're angry!

the things I cannot control, the things life throws at you with a curve, testing you, alerting you of life's ever-changing ways. My biggest fear resides in my very own heart: the fear of losing my father, a fear Earth himself has already faced. It is a fear that has come to reality within his life as he looked it in the eyes like a demon, a demon who took his father away.

Will this same demon one day take my father away, too?

What will I do when it does?

Will I really have the strength to overcome it, as Ernesto states so confidently?

When the Princess flees to learn the world, she does not forget about the roots from where she comes. The King and Queen who began her journey. Her mother and father—no, she doesn't forget them, not even for a wild moment.

"*Bueno*, Deanna." Ernesto's voice snaps me back into the light. "*Tus novios. No son novios.* ¡*SON AVENTURAS!*"[72] Ernesto slams his fist onto the table, not breaking eye contact with me, his mug filled with *café* quivering. Bruno, who lies on the floor next to Ernesto, raises his head in shock.

I do the same.

"Now go to bed and pray. Pray for both your parents and your brothers and stop dating adventures. They are too ugly for you! ¡*Son feos para una mujer como usted!*"[73]

With this Ernesto laughs a great laugh, breaking the tension of the moment. His elbows are back on the table, his fingertips pressed together to form a tipi.

I think I'm laughing as well, though I'm not so sure.

***

---

72 Your boyfriends, they are not your partners, they are adventures.

73 They're ugly for a woman like you!

The first lesson of Earth is the lesson of judgment. Who are we to judge another human without having walked an inch in their shoes? Judgment is way too prevalent and common to be productive. Our earthly judgments of what we think is right and wrong are based upon our personal life experiences and don't frequently take into consideration another person's hardships and sufferings. The element of Earth asks us to come back to square one where it all began and where it will all end. Right here. Right now. Earth asks us to be curious and discover why people do the things they do instead of judging them. We can never learn from others if we're already blocking them without knowing just who they are, or who they can be.

The second lesson of Earth is the lesson of our own roots, where we come from, our family, and our tribe. We all have one, whether we like it or not. We all come from somewhere, a dark, shady history or a fantastic childhood. The spent days of our youth largely determine how we interact with the world once we are out of our parents' kingdom. Element Earth teaches us where we come from is not coincidence, but crucial. There are many things we learn from our original roots which carry onward in life, and if left unresolved they can cause demons to arise later on. Earth also tells us that whatever happened, is not your fault, but certainly your destiny to grow from.

The third lesson of Earth is the lesson of humility. This goes hand in hand with the role of the Jester. The Jester, whose main purpose is to entertain, is not ashamed when being laughed at, but humiliated in a way that brings a certain humbleness to heaven. Humiliation is different than what we've been taught. It allows one to ease themselves into their human-hood, to make mistakes, and to learn the lessons of life. It asks one to forgive and be forgiven. Earth is humble and will humble you by testing you, by laughing at you, and by seeing how you play with both the dark and the light in your life.

***

After four weeks nestled in Ernesto's home, I'm moving onward.

I board the bus with a stamped ticket. Easing my mind to the sounds of the road, I think of his face. The joyous one. The hurt one. The paranoid one. If there's something I've learned through his presence, it's that humans yearn to be understood, not shamed.

Twelve hours later the bus stops at a main station in Guatemala City. I hop inside a taxi van. I think of his smile and how it lit up a whole room, how it lit up my whole life. I think of the pain he had to overcome to wear this smile, the smile that's his only victory.

The taxi van stops at the central market in Antigua. I adjust my backpack and start walking.

Past the water fountain.

Past Maximón's cave.

Past the churches and their bells.

I walk right up to that hole in the wall hostel.

There I see him in the same exact spot where I met him on my first night, same chair and everything.

But he's different to me now because I know his depths, his secrets, and his story.

I place a firm hand on his shoulder.

He turns around.

His face is shocked.

"*¿Nena..?*"

"*Vamos, mi amor.*"

"*¿Donde?*'"

"*Vamos.*"

I grab his hand and guide him to the streets, down the city, and up the stairs to the artist that awaits us.

***

I bring the lined notebook paper to my puckered lips. Gracing it ever so slightly, I make my mark and pull it away. Earth grabs the paper, observing each detailed crevice of the kiss.

"*Otra vez,*" he demands.[74]

I twist the cheap tube of fuchsia lipstick and bring its tip to my lips for a third round. This time I pucker just a little less, keeping my mouth slightly open as I make contact once again. Pulling away the notebook paper, I see my third attempt alongside the first and second. He takes the paper with an approving smirk and passes it to the tattoo artist.

"*Eso.*"

"*¿Seguro?*"[75]

"*Sí.*"

I take my royal seat across the room, wearing my crown as Queen, and watch as Earth removes his polka dot shirt. Over his head and onto my lap it flies, exposing the smooth caramel skin of his back.

"*Aquí?*" the tattoo artist asks and points to a spot on his upper left shoulder.

I peek my head to get a better view.

---

74   Again.

75   Are you sure?

"*Exactamente.*"

"*¿Seguro?*"

"*Si.*"

The pen buzzes and makes contact with his shoulder.

I watch my lips appear, from body to paper to skin.

A kiss to keep until death.

And even shortly after.

FIRE

THE MODERN-DAY MONK

———

The door does not sway, nor open, as the narrow frame of an elder woman enters inside *La Cocina*.[76] She takes each step as if she's existing in slow motion. Her worn slippers grace the floor, one behind the other, adorned with tricolored flowers. Over her chest hangs a robe lavished in the embroidery of the dead. Her hair is silky grey, like that of a Persian cat, resting in two lengthy braids alongside her exposed *calavera*.[77]

Nearing the end of October, upon tradition, this old grandmother and many others like her make their long and silent journey from the realm of the dead and onto the streets of the living. Each year, the Deads come embellished in colored threads, their costumes of culture hanging over their exposed skeletal frames. They don't come to haunt the living, but to simply be celebrated. They wander the streets as their thriving lineage honors *El Día de los Muertos* year after year.[78]

———

76 The kitchen.

77 Skull

78 The day of the dead. A holiday celebrated each year in Mexico to honor the past ancestors.

Some Deads bring with them gifts of the unknown, little blessings and such.

A few Deads bring hysteria and pain.

But the Deads that are the most revered are the Deads who bring their stories.

As she makes her way through the colorful kitchen, a large, leather-bound journal is spotted underneath the arms of La Abuela.[79] The book is dusty, as she hasn't revealed her stories to the living in decades.

Oh, the stories La Abuela has to tell!

They speak of her family, ancestors, and lineage, and they're all located precisely in this wonderful and voluminous book.

La Abuela decides that this year, it's time to share a story.

She takes her sweet time arriving to the solitary table located smack in the middle of the kitchen. Who would place a table in the center of a room like this? With each everlasting shuffle, the clock strikes another second. Twenty-three seconds later, La Abuela takes a comfortable seat, resting her stiff bones.

Her eyeless gaze hesitates to lift upward, but when it does her audience of one, sitting on a chair directly in front of her, is greeted by sustenance and antiquity. She grins a grin of mischief as she parts the leather-bound journal in half, ready to release her secrets.

"*Lista, mi amor*?" she asks.[80]

Yes, she's dead, and yes, she can talk! How else could she recount her stories?

---

79 Grandma

80 Are you ready, my love?

Her single onlooker doesn't answer, but simply nods without taking her eyes off of old Abuela's charm.

She wipes the surface of the vulnerable exposed page with the edge of her exotic shawl.

"This is the sweet face I remember." Her memories activate as she presents the pages' contents to the living world.

Turning the journal around to face her curious viewer, the page vividly comes alive and a story begins with Abuela's voice recounting the details.

Back when armadillos roamed the deserts freely and hawks looped tenfold in the sky, there stood a young man in a central Mexican village who had a vision. This vision lead the young man on a quest—a quest for a better life, a quest of courage. He fled the familiar and rural streets of his hometown and took to the unknown route which called many souls toward it: the route to *La Frontera,* the border.

Over dusty hills and parched landscapes, he wandered on this trail. Through the thicket and bush his feet paced. The sun beat ferociously on his back, yet his perspiration pushed him forward. The young man weaseled his way from village to village, feeding himself off *la comida* prepared by the hands of *muchas abuelas.*

One day, he arrived. He walked across *La Frontera* blinded by the light of hope, as if entering the glistening gates of Heaven. He already saw the new life that was awaiting him just on the other side.

The young man sharpened his life skills in this new world where everything hung so modified. The animated streets of central Mexico were replaced by orderly stoplights, professional police officers, and weekly paychecks. It took him time and reluctance to adjust, but the young man never faltered. *Nunca.* Though it wasn't easy, he took credit where it was due, asked questions, received criticism, and devoted his time nonstop to build the life of security and influence this new land promised.

Now, far away from his origins, he took permanent residence in a small community located just far enough from the edges of Atlanta, Georgia. This is where he found prosperity awaiting him. He quickly surrounded himself with *muchos amigos*, a successful business, his loving wife, and their four wide-eyed, provided-for children.

Old Abuela pauses and looks down at the page in front of her. The page showcases a worn photograph of four small children standing close together. She doesn't breathe, for she doesn't need to, but the living audience in front of her takes many short breaths as the story lingers in the air. After enough hesitance, La Abuela begins once more, speaking in an even slower and mysterious tone.

"His wife gifted him with three vastly different sons and a graceful daughter that every father wishes to have."

She points her boney finger to the face of the oldest child in the photograph. "The first son was firm like a rock."

Her pointer slides over just a quarter inch. "The second son harnessed a joyful personality."

Old Abuela pauses for an anticipating breath as her finger glides toward the most fragile and pale child in the aged photograph.

She taps the page three times as she speaks. "The third son was the one whose life held a different plan for."

At this, the once lively page of the journal goes blank as the last sentence leaves her arid voice, tossing the audience into a quiet anxiety. Old Abuela takes her time glancing around the entire kitchen, taking in the colors and decor, before choosing to speak again. Without moving a finger, the open journal turns its very own pages, livening up again, presenting another photo which depicts the third son as a newborn child.

The story pursues.

"Look at the baby." Old Abuela points to the photo of the small and frail newborn nestled in a hospital bed.

"He arrived before his birth. He was destined for the late summer but came on the cusp of Leo."

"Do you know what that means, *mi amor*? He was eager to enter this earth. That third son of his was born premature and so he was presented with many challenges the first two sons hadn't been."

Every summer, when the bulk of the family traveled back to Mexico, this small child did just fine with adjusting socially to the lesser-developed streets, but his body didn't. No one in the family noticed—not his mother nor father and especially not the frail third son himself.

Let's go back to the father now, shall we?

While raising his children, the ambitious father began to instill his entrepreneurial mentality into their minds, especially the third son whose big brown eyes revered this father of his as a king. *Un rey del sol.*[81]

The page turns, revealing an animated picture of the young son, eight years old, walking into a restaurant with a blue knapsack hunched over his petite frame.

Each day after school the third son arrived at the family business with his books still upon his back. Without complaints or hesitation, he would find his way to the cleaning products in the back closet and begin wiping down table after table behind every dining customer.

---

81 A ray of the sun

Old Abuela takes a moment to observe his face in the newly appearing photograph. In just one swift turn of the page, the third son jumps from an eight-year-old frail child to a twenty-year-old frail man. Old Abuela continues with a voice that grows intense.

Thousands of customers and hundreds of tables later, the third son stood tall and proud as the new owner of his father's precious business. He was taught how to interact with the employees, managing a team of people who he built a relationship with since his childhood.

He learned the minor and major details of running the business, from top to bottom, in the same way his father had done. He stocked the shelves and dealt with hard-to-please customers. He stabilized the front and back of this fast-paced environment day after day after day after day...

The voice of Old Abuela trails off into a simmer, as though she's lost her train of thought. The pages of the journal suddenly fade, no longer holding the magic they presented just seconds prior.

The lone audience of one, who is so naturally invested in the story, finally looks up to see Old Abuela frozen in time. Not knowing what to do, the audience speaks aloud anxiously.

"*Abuelita, que te pasa?*"[82]

Abuela shakes her head in a reluctant manner, not relating what she's experiencing within her soul.

"*Abuelita, dime, que te pasa?*"

"Pues, *mi amor. No me gusta esta parte de la historia,*"[83] Old Abuela speaks aloud as a tear rolls down her *calavera*.

---

82 Granny, what's wrong?

83 Well, my love, I don't like this part of the story.

The heart of her audience now grows sympathetic.

"*Todo esta bien Abuelita. Necesito saber.* I want to know what happens next." [84]

"*Bien.*"

As her movements and voice come to life once more, the pages in her journal flip wildly, revealing an image of a young and sickly man dressed in an orderly uniform. His frame is thin, his skin a pale-yellow hue. He stands in a commercial kitchen, surrounded by coworkers. Even though his eyes speak of death, one can see they hold *fuerza*.[85] There is still strength in his eyes.

"You see, *mi amor*, he had a lot of responsibility upon his shoulders—*mucho*. Everyone around him started to look up to him more, demanding his attention, which only added to that weight. He developed a team of people who respected his orders in the same way they respected his father's."

As the third son's relationship with his father improved, so did his career and finances. His career was on an upward elevator to success and financial liberation, while his health and personal well-being fell down a rapid and spiraling hole. These two contrasting aspects held steady for a long, long time.

Abuela shakes her loose *calavera* in a sad manner.

This third son—he was in pain. Aye! *Que dolor!* The pain was constant and inexplicable. His yearly visits to rural Mexico and past sufferings as a premature child had affected his health down the road. This dangerous combination created the weakened immune system of the sick twenty-year-old man you see here in the photograph.

---

84 It's okay grandma, I need to know.

85 Strength

Torn between his two worlds, the third son remained steady in his noble position as the new owner while being thrown pills and pharmaceuticals from all directions. His visits to many doctors offered a potential shimmer of hope, yet each ended with another night of nausea, fever, and hot flashes.

The journal shifts pages and casts an image of three different men wearing long, white professional coats. Their voices come through the photographs, one at a time.

"Parasites," one claims.

"Acid reflux," the second one chimes in.

"Some bacterial things," suggests the last doctor.

The third son had visited with many health doctors like this throughout his life, yet the doctors never asked the important question—the question that would reveal the truth behind his mysterious illness.

Old Abuela halts her story and looks up toward her audience, who is patiently waiting. The clock on the wall ticks two or three times before the silence is broken.

"What was the special question, *Abuelita*?"

"*Ah. Que bueno. Quieres saber.*"[86]

"Those *pinche doctors* never asked him, 'What is your diet like?' No one knew this, *mi amor*, but the food he had been consuming his entire life was the devil behind the symptoms of his suffering."

The page transforms again and illustrates yet another photograph of the sick young man.

"*Mira, mi amor, que malo.*"[87]

---

86 How good. You want to know.

87 Look, my love, how bad.

Weak, pale, thin, and burnt-out from the long hours at the business, the third son reached a breaking point of despair. He had not a clue what to do with himself and his pain. Yet he lived his life as he did, a busy young man in agony and constant physical hurt.

Without warning, the journal slams shut with such a brutal force that dust is launched across the table. Old Abuela pounds both of her boney hands on the table.

"We are done! *Basta!*" She stands up with such rapidity it leaves her audience in shock.

"*Abuelita! A donde vas?*"[88]

Before the voice is considered, Old Abuela simply disappears, leaving behind her luminous journal. Vibrating with the energy of Old Abuela's mystical stories, the desperate audience is left alone with the journal.

"I need to know the rest of the story *now!* Journal, *por favor*, show me the rest!"

The journal hesitates, wiggles around, and gives a sigh of reluctance before opening and exposing its contents once again.

***

To look inside the journal of the Dead is a dangerous feat everyone knows of. Without a narrator, it's too easy to lose sight of the story and get lost in its flames, making one go mad with curiosity and suspension. But tonight, we have a risk-taker. Tonight, we'll see what the journal will share that Old Abuela will not.

---

88 Where are you going?

The journal shows an illuminated picture of the third son, pale as ever, placing a small and colorful piece of paper underneath his tongue. After this, the images change rapidly, depicting an entirely different world.

Mesmerizing images of shapes and symbols float freely out of the journal page. Every color that exists in the realm of the universe shines out through the thin pages and into the entire *Cocina*. Mythical creatures flash by, as do religious figures of all kinds. The dancing molecules of every image are constantly transforming. A hard-to-hear sound emits from the journal, as if someone is whispering through the page.

The audience listens keenly, turning her head and placing her right ear to the book. Her hands come to her mouth, attempting to not explode of laughter, as the sounds enters her brain, making sense of the imagery.

The sounds spell out three letters.

"L-S-D."

The trip gradually ends, leaving the audience sitting back in her chair, arms crossed, awaiting what comes next.

The journal flashes a series of pictures that the audience has to make sense of herself. The first is of the third son handing his father a set of keys. The second is of him preparing and eating a meal. The third photograph displays the young man with vitality and health. The fourth photo showcases the third son and a friend leaving in a large white vehicle. The fifth is a still photograph of nature. The sixth shows the big white vehicle once more.

Now, the seventh photograph stays for a long time. It's of the third son, of course, sitting in a posture of meditation upon the floor. His shoulders are relaxed, his chin slightly tucked into his chest. Through the image, his torso moves up and down with each breath. His skin is not pale but has a healthy glow. His frame is not thin, but filled in. Something about him in this photograph is altered, as he sits peacefully in this meditative posture.

The audience watches in awe, her jitters calming down. She feels as if she was brought on a wild roller coaster ride, between Old Abuela's intensity, the story, the photographs themselves, and her own inner emotions. *Aye aye aye!* What is she to make of these series of photos, though? What did this last photograph want to share with her?

The audience leans forward in her chair, bringing her face as close as possible to the breathing image in front of her. Yet before she can ask any follow-up questions, the journal slowly turns a page for the final time. As the photograph of the now healthy young man seated in meditation falls, a title is spilled out from across the paper.

"Modern-Day Monk."

"Oh. I get it..." The lone audience looks down and places her hands over her heart. Basking in the realization, she smiles to herself, entering a place of stillness and understanding, but her silence is broken when Old Abuela reappears on the seat out in front of her.

"So you see now, *mi amor,* why this story is so special for you? My dear grandson, the Modern-Day Monk, chose a different path for himself. It's not one we talk about often, as his decision hurt the entire family when he fled from us. He ran away, vanished out of thin air, so that he could discover himself. He may not have followed in the tradition your grandfather wanted, but he was able to heal his body and thus transform his life. He's broken through many veils for our family, and you, *mi amor,*" Old Abuela's compassionate presence grows tenfold, "will do the same."

With that, the journal, Old Abuela, and the story disappears, leaving the young girl—the audience of one—forever grateful to know the true story of her dear uncle, the third son.

ONCE UPON A BENCH

I step out of my mother's car to grab my items. They're a scant few: books, yoga mat, ukulele, and a duffle bag with modest clothing. My mother parks the car, assists me, and bids me farewell yet again. She drives off, and I make my way toward my friend's vehicle across the parking lot, lugging all these items. Nancy is currently working, busy as a bee, so I slump my comfortable body against the passenger tire, take out my ukulele, and strum a jolly tune.

In the glistening sun I sing to myself underneath the New Jersey spring sky. I'm right back in the place of my birth, good ol' Brick Township, but never for long. Reverse culture shock happens, but it happens fast. Once you notice it, it's most likely already gone. But the worst part about it is the food withdrawal from the place you have recently left behind, the food withdrawal and the adventure withdrawal. With very little on my mind I caress the strings, enchanting my own self and worrying onlookers who exit the library.

It's been well over a year since I've visited my family, and each time I do I slip out just as quietly as I slipped in, tip-toeing off, to my father's dismay, into another distant land. Here I go again. I can't get enough. Nope, I must disappoint my parents once more. Though this time I won't be going as far as Hawaii, Thailand, or Guatemala City. I'll only be a hop, skip, and a jump away, hidden among trees and corn crop in the rural back fields of yawn provoking Pennsylvania.

Okay, okay, I'll get off my Jersey high horse. Pennsylvania has great things to offer someone, like haunted historical sites, for instance, or copious amounts of corn, not to mention the thought-provoking Amish culture. Yes, Pennsylvania is a land rich in itself, taking its lowest rank among the tristate area and accepting the fate of its land-locked misfortune.

There is reason for such a drastic lowering in intensity, and that reason is I need a goddamn break.

For the past five years I flew, arrived, hitchhiked, wheeled, walked, and crawled from city to city. You can really start to see my exhaustion by the roughness of my face, the thick edges of my hips and the few protruding grey hairs atop my head. I'm in need of a reset. The traveler's road is a wild one, and just because you get out alive doesn't necessarily mean what hasn't killed you made you stronger.

That's the reason I'm going to rural Pennsylvania.

That's the reason I'm going to an ashram.

And no.

It has nothing to do with Elizabeth Gilbert's *Eat, Pray, Love.*

I was holding a stained piece of cardboard with the Khmer alphabet on it, hitching rides in Cambodia before I knew that book existed.

Rumor has it that on the side of the road in a town no one knows about sits an abandoned school. This is a jail-cell-looking building, and quite nearly acted as one back in the day when young misbehaved boys were sent there to be looked after with a sharp eye. The school had its own security guards and teachers who attempted to discipline the rowdy students. Whatever happened after that is a mystery—to me at least, as the building lost its purpose and sat untouched for some time.

Until one day, the building was located by a middle-aged couple with an eager eye. They had a vision in mind, and the building provided access to it. Their vision wasn't peculiar or bizarre. It was a vision most folks have but just don't know. Their vision was that of community. They wanted to fill the building from bottom to top with love, resurrecting its purpose.

They planned to do this through the teachings of the now-popular yoga. They envisioned classrooms, a cafeteria, and a big ol' kitchen. They envisioned hosting classes in meditation, yoga, and training yoga teachers all the while serving the surrounding community robust and healthy farm-to-table food. They envisioned laughter, music, gardening, and growth of the soul. They envisioned a family.

I'm now about to walk into that living vision of community. This is why I sit, strumming my ukulele like a melodramatic fool against the tire of Nancy's car in the bashful sun. Nancy has been a solid rock in the life of Deanna. Funny little fact: Nancy, although thirty years my senior, was my first yoga student. Immediately drawn to my delightfully charming charisma, she approached me one day after class and the rest became history. Nancy was inspired and thus went on to study yoga on her own, attending the ashram where she is now about to deliver me.

***

"I see you fitting right in, Deanna. You'll love this group."

Nancy speaks to me as she turns down the traffic-less highway.

No traffic in New Jersey can mean one of two things:

1. You're hallucinating.
2. You are headed to Pennsylvania.

"Oh, yeah? What makes you say that?"

"Well, they're like you." She looks over at me like the adoring woman she is. "They're adventurous and spiritual; they cook and grow their own food. Doesn't that say Deanna all over it?"

"I guess so, but are they crazy like me? I've never been able to behave myself in church for, like, an hour, let alone an ashram for a few months. I don't wanna embarrass my father or anything like that."

Hearing my Jersey accent heighten, Nancy laughs and shakes her head.

"You're too funny, Deanna. I guess you'll find out."

***

She turns down a road that whips through the passing scenery of tall oaks and lively foliage. The road winds and curves, not stopping for anyone or anything. Without any indication of slowing down, she takes a smooth turn into an empty parking lot, letting her car slowly ease on up to the base of a small concrete flight of steps.

"This is it, Dee."

Twisting the keys toward her, the car murmurs to a rattling stop and the hum of the road finally ceases. I take stock of my surroundings—big building, bricks, beige, in the middle of nowhere. It's definitely not Guatemala. If Guatemala sees in rainbows, this building is color-blind, and it's color-blinding me. I rub my eyes to get a better look. Where are the colorful Tibetan flags and bronze buddhas? Where are the mandalas painted on the side of the building? Where is the painted hippie bus?

Nowhere to be found, apparently.

I hesitantly follow her with my meager items up the concrete steps and through a wide-open door leading to a slightly more colorful hallway.

My sense of smell is alerted. Someone is cooking something. It reminds me of my own hunger. Like a dog on duty, I inhale the aromas, making guesses as to what it could be. Curry and rice? Dal? Maybe chana masala? My mind draws up a feast of fantasy, distracting me from anything else in the hallway.

I locate the bronze Buddha, but this one is a little different than I had in mind. I walk over to the statue and touch upon its metallic finish. The deity has two pairs of arms which twist and wiggle like serpents. It stands on one foot while the other is kicked across its body. I trace its figure and observe what is happening below it. A young naked baby with the face of an old man is stationed on its hands and knees, allowing the Buddha to dance on top of its back.

"That's the Dancing Shiva standing on the Old Man of Ignorance."

An unfamiliar voice comes from down the long hallway, followed by a plethora of humans.

Well, not *that* many humans.

Just four humans.

They each tell me their birth name and their spiritual given name, offer me a hug, and welcome me into the ashram. I scratch my head, already confused with who is who, and still distraught over the Old Man of Ignorance. I'm then left standing in between a circle of excited yogis whose names I cannot remember for the life of me. I slip my hands into my pockets and retreat just a step, perching against the wall. Just as quickly as they came, they disappear, only leaving behind a tall middle-aged woman with long blonde hair, who goes by the name Michelle.

"We're happy to have you here. Springtime means lots of work in the gardens and we'll need you out there. I hope you don't mind the rain." Her face radiates joy. "I've heard quite a lot about you, Deanna. I've awaited this day for a long time."

I smile and nod.

"It's great to be here."

She begins informing me about the lifestyle here, describing the gardens in full detail and the outline of my days to come. We get into a deep conversation about her travels in Australia and mine in Latin America. I'm really liking this chick. She's got spunk. She speaks fast, is easy to make laugh, and tells stories with a flare I appreciate.

I stay perched against the wall, listening to her chant on about her encounter with a unicyclist in Tennessee, when a discrete door behind me swings open and a young man steps out. Michelle catches his movement out of the corner of her eye and brings all of her prior attention to a brash halt and settles it on him.

"Oh!" she shrieks. "Have you two met yet?"

He walks all but three steps toward us in a very relaxed and grounded manner. I go to hug him because, well, that's what people do in ashrams, isn't it? As I step back from the embrace, something strange arises within me. It feels like a token of poison, or a pinch of delight. Whatever it is, it's perplexing and makes me feel as if a magnetic pulsation is pushing me away from him, not pulling me toward him.

Resistance.

Sweet and beautiful resistance.

I open my mouth.

"Nice to meet you."

He bows, further revealing his shaved head, and walks away.

***

I have the intuition of a woman: strong and without reason.

Why does it come when it comes?

I don't know.

It's not necessarily looking to protect me but sends signals which allow me time to prepare for what's to come. It doesn't take me long to identify the strange sensation and the wavering intuition. But why would I resist someone I don't yet know? Or yet, maybe I do know him, on a deeper and more soulful level, and that's where the resistance arose from. Anyway, whatever it was, it was present, and it was real.

Inside of the spacious cafeteria I dip my bag of herbal tea into the steaming water. I lift it up and let it slowly sink down into the warmth, watching colors stain the clear water. The sun is set and night-time prevails. I've received my grand tour of the long and vacant building and my belongings are tucked away neatly in my new sleeping quarters. I've met everyone there is to meet, including the founders of the ashram.

My five minutes of solitude are over when the door to the cafeteria opens. Under the dim set lighting, I watch out of the corner of my eye as a figure casually enters the room and sweeps right past me. My eyes stay downward to watch the steam rise from my cup. I don't exchange words with this person. I just stand awkwardly, feeling as if I've been ripped out of my hiding spot.

He stands beside me now. Taking the hot tea kettle, he pours water into a matching mug right next to mine. The silence in the room is long, drawn-out, and unnecessary. It's like he's trying to prove a point through his calmness and his silence. Little does he know the silence screams louder than a maniac. I try to ease up as the resistance in my body rises again, muting my mind that keeps thinking, "Would ya go away already?"

His gaze is upon me; I feel it.

It burns the side of my face.

I wait a moment before lifting my head to meet his brown eyes.

"Do you want to go outside?" he asks, his voice coming out monotone and neutral.

I pick up my mug and inhale the rising steam, burning hot on my damp hands.

"Sure," I reply, matching his austere tone.

***

The hot mug is the only thing comforting about this moment, and the stars that are visible overhead, though I must admit there is nothing special about them this evening. For a long while, no one speaks. I sit on one end of the bench, as he exists on the other. Off into the distance we stare, sipping, like long-lived folks on a wooden porch.

I decide to take the leap.

"So how long have you been here?"

I watch his face.

His eyes close and stay that way, fluttering ever so slightly in their place like a plastic doll with such features. It takes him a long time to reply, and in the midst of his solitude I revert my attention back out in front of me.

"So, I've been here since last May." His voice is still monotone.

"A year?" I ask for validation. Why I care about these details is beyond me.

"Yeah," he separates his answer with an exhale, "a year."

"How long do you think you'll stay?" I ask again out of nothingness.

Once more, I watch his face as he gracefully takes a sip of his tea, closes his eyes for a second time, and searches for the answer in the corners of his mind.

"We spoke about me staying until the end of June." Monotone again.

"That's a long time from now." I pause in my reply. "Anything can happen from now until then."

He absorbs my statement. "Yeah. I understand. That could change. It's just an idea."

We both return to our teas, sipping in silence.

He never asked, yet I decide to share with him about my recent explorations in Latin America, speaking out of discomfort rather than excitement. He listens like an old man on a porch with nothing better to do, sipping and nodding after each sentence, not contributing anything after I finish my display.

My resistance toward him is now transforming into a curious suspicion. He's certainly hard to read, and why the hell did he bring me outside on this damp bench? I question if it's his way of flirting with me. If so, he's doing a very poor job. Don't think I assume this out of ignorance. I assume this because I'm a lady and he is a man. When men ask ladies to go somewhere in private with them, an awareness must arise. I've been around the world far too much at this point to not know this.

Oh, shit, he's speaking now!

Let's hear what this dude has to say.

"Life is the ever-unfolding of the journey that is not yet known to us." He finishes this Buddha-like statement and returns his focus back to the night sky.

That's it?

That's all he has to say?

Well goddamn, I want a refund!

I surrender once more to the conversation, trying very hard to keep the flame alive.

"Yes, it certainly is. The people we meet along the way are truly what makes life worth living. Sometimes, without knowing it, we meet people who are destined to change our lives."

As the lukewarm tea enters my mouth, a flash of realization is thrown at me from my intuition.

"Catch this," it hollers.

Oh, fuck.

No! No.

Not again.

I'm not ready for this.

I don't want it again—not him.

Can I stop it from happening?

My intuition is too strong. I already know, already sense, already have a clear visual that this very simple, monotonous, and perplexing man before me is going to take on the role of another romance. How the hell does this happen *everywhere* I go? Now I understand why the resistance was so present earlier today. I'm meant to learn something from him.

Even though I don't really want to.

He speaks again, breaking my mind out of its war.

"Yes. All we must do is surrender to the unity that is within us all."

He finishes his last sip of tea and stands up, holding the posture of a perfected Thai Chi master.

"Don't spend all your time indoors."

He bows his head slightly and walks across the courtyard and into the door from which we came, leaving me with an empty mug in my hands and a mind full of chatter.

I look up toward the sky.

Really?

Him?

But I already know the answer.

ONE MORE TIME
FOR GOOD MEASURE

———

Sometimes a romance becomes so nonchalant, so casual and easy to access, it actually starts to put a bad taste in one's mouth. It becomes like a piece of gum that's been over-chewed, but just keeps getting chewed. The only juices remaining are stale saliva left behind from a once tastier moment.

How can one be honest with themselves and acknowledge this unproductive pattern in a world where romance is all the rage? People use apps to locate soulmates and screens that show them faces of potential enchanters. If only they could take a moment to just stop, hit the brakes, and call it a day for once.

Some do, but others, like me, do not.

Because we haven't yet learned how.

We haven't created the proper boundaries.

I turn over in my bed.

The sparkling white sheets make me feel as if I'm too dirty to be sleeping upon them. Lava runs through my veins, creeping and building with rage all from the interactions that transpired on the bench. Tonight was my very first night in an ashram. Does this *really* need to happen everywhere I go?

Really?

It's like a curse I cannot expel.

The second I arrive somewhere, it seems it's always destined—written in the stars, fixated in time—I will just happen to "meet" someone. It's become unquestionably obvious upon these initial encounters, but at this point I'm not sure if my spirit sends the signals as warning or warmth. Whichever it is, I'm troubled by this pattern that haunts me like a ghost.

A level of honesty must be obtained for one to realize the reality of having back-to-back enchanters. If they can't stop the eruption of a romance in time, "here we go again" becomes the mantra. This is a common pattern playing out for men and women alike, and before they can turn around to stop an expanding explosion, they'll find the sweltering ground beginning to rumble beneath their feet.

What are our options when we cannot stop an outbreak from occurring?

What can we do when the thrill of attraction controls our every morsel of being?

When we have no control over the explosions of lust is when romance becomes a tiresome quest. There's no use in kicking and screaming; the volcano has a life of its own. Certainly, we can just surrender, toss ourselves into the flames, and watch our little hearts burn. Surrender to the lessons that we must, *apparently,* learn.

I'll tell you the truth.

I'm tired of meeting this "someone."

I'm vexed by romance, perplexed by love.

It doesn't take a three-eyed psychic to see I no longer have control over these occurrences and I, in fact, never did. As you've been witnessing, along the way I indifferently stumbled into them like the secret ingredient to a bubbling pot of the witch's special brew. One minute I see the pot bubbling from afar. Now, a tornado of ingredients simmer around me: lust, passion, pleasure, potatoes, and Deanna.

I recall one evening during my early travels in Latin America when I was enjoying dinner with a lovely blond-haired, blue-eyed Canadian man. We were both backpacking, and our paths happen to mesh at that moment. At this time in my life, my emotions took on the resemblance of a limp log drifting in the murky waters of my mind. I couldn't get away. On and on I recalled stories and upsets to this calm man about my previous lovers.

At one point during our dinner, his strikingly blue eyes met mine.

Then came his strikingly true words.

"You have a problem with ex-boyfriends."

His words first came like a gentle slap across the face, and later came like a freight train of truth. I kept my trap shut for the rest of the evening, not because of offense but because an outside source was seeing my illusion for what it really was: a reality. Unlike Ernesto's lighthearted words, the impact of this young man's statement got straight to the point.

"I do, my friend, have a problem, but I don't, my friend, have any control over it."

The embarrassment of this defeat continued to sink deep into me like a low-grade virus, coming to the surface only when I was exposed to a pathogenic truth which lowered my spiritual immunity.

Whereas Ernesto gracefully handed me a lighter in hopes that I would use it to illuminate my "boyfriend/adventure" issue, the blue-eyed Canadian man shone a light directly on my face, instantly exposing just one aspect of my issue. It's my responsibility to locate the other aspects. I'm well aware of the constant urgent mission to fill in the empty gaps of myself with a masculine counterpart, but I'm not aware of how to reverse it, or if reversing it is something within my control.

You see, I was born woman.

I'll be honest in saying that I desire nothing more than a union where I can share my bountiful harvest of love.

Women are the masters of nourishment, nurturing, and healing.

It's why we have wombs, ya know?

We take something which needs growth and embody it in our energetic womb space, holding onto it like a baby of our very own. Whereas men want to "fix" things, women want to "heal" things, and more frequently than not those things are people. And heal them we will! The whole damn world if we must. Women must strive to realize we can only make the world a better place when we leave problems outside of our wombs and bodies and work with them from there.

It's tricky.

Why?

Because many women have never been taught this.

So we must teach ourselves how to be in the world without the world being inside of us, overcoming the years of suppression, manipulation, pain, suffering, and injustice.

Then we must go on to teach men how to treat a woman who is whole and how to respect boundaries so we can find a partner who matches our wisdom, reign and royalty.

So we can find a partnership where not one, but two can thrive.

I suppose this is a lesson I have not yet overcome.

So welcome, Fire. Please, show me what I've been missing.

THE SHORT PATH

I don't know how the walls are coming down, or maybe I do. It might be by consuming so many meals or sitting side by side in silence. Or maybe it's happening subliminally during our morning meditation sessions where we, once again, sit together daily in a withdrawn state. My aversion toward Fire is beginning to ease, and I'm unsure if I like it.

Fire speaks in a strange manner, one which makes conversations gracefully perplexing. His words come like forlorn afterthoughts, void of substance, void of imagery, and void of perception. Maybe he feels uncomfortable around me, but if he does, he'll never show it because he is always at ease.

Or that's what he wants you think.

Factitious joy follows him around and his aura is always contained, never stepping out of boundary, remaining just a calm flicker. Like a sacred fire that cannot be left to burn out, these flames have a constant observer and caretaker: his own self. His strange presence doesn't harbor emotions, but a lack thereof, making you deeply question if he is enlightened or robotic.

The way Fire attends to himself is like a sober elderly man who is not yet elder. People may refer to this as being wise or mindful. I'm learning to call it meticulous. I discreetly observe him during our lunches, when we join around the cafeteria table. We stuff our mouths with garden fresh veggies, dal, and rice, yet Fire refuses to intake one single morsel of food.

Why?

Because he's committed to spending twenty-three hours a day fasting, not consuming anything aside from water or ginger tea, and one hour in a state of caloric intake, that is, consuming everything left in the fridge.

Everything.

I wearily observe him while he works in the gardens. He wears a straw hat to protect his delicate pale skin. Out in nature he communes, using his body in the most efficient way, so as not to waste any energy or put strain on his fragile muscles and tender ligaments. He bends down attentively to pick up loads of hay, keeping his gait in complete alignment during the process as if he were programmed this way.

I observe him in conversation, or better yet while he allows the other person to speak. He stands always with his legs apart, hands clutching each other across his chest as if forming a mudra.[89] He graciously nods his head up and down to express his elaborate role of participation. During group discussions he listens but never shares, snickers but never cackles, speaks but never expresses.

I don't forget to observe the way I feel during these observations of the strange man who lives alongside me. Perplexing though he is, there's a stature of wholeness, innocence, and maybe even simplicity in him. In the beginning I wanted

---

89 A symbolic gesture practiced with the hands or fingers in Hinduism or Buddhism

to shake him, thrash him out of his forced trance. He's stubborn with his truths and openly closed off to outside opinions. I see this as a game—a game I want to play, but only to change the rules.

I've begun to slip inside his mind, ever so slightly, with my rash Jersey accent and my unapologetic ways, cracking ill-advised jokes, sharing rowdy stories, and pushing his hard-to-locate buttons. I want to see what the flames do when I throw all I've got into them. I want to see them crackle, snap, and blaze. I want to watch the flames expand to a point of no return. I want to tempt temptation itself.

It's working.

For now, I observe him laughing.

I observe him eating breakfast (for heaven's sake, breakfast!).

I observe him observing me with his energy, his eyes, and his aura.

They all observe me.

This is when I stop observing him.

This is when my wall comes down, allowing the Trojan horse to enter—destruction in disguise.

***

Knees digging into the wet grass, I reach across the ground and grab for a ripe tomato. Holding the heirloom in my palm, I notice its palette of color. It's wrinkled in all the right places, seamless, and juicy. Now that's a tomato, folks. Up the driveway, my attention is caught, landing on a tall man I've never seen before. He's casually approaching, carrying a cardboard box. I follow behind Michelle to meet the gentle-faced man.

"Hi. Can we help you?" Michelle's high voice calls out to him.

He blushes, a smile squinting his eyes.

"Hey, I thought you would want these."

He sets the box on a picnic table.

"I'm cleaning out my house. Went through a long phase of reading scriptures and spiritual texts. I don't see the public library having any use for them."

All the ashramites are huddled together, peeking inside the box into a world of pages, completely delighted by the unplanned occurrence.[90] It's not every day a fine-looking man brings a fine-looking box of books to the ashram. He's tall, with a sculpted face and taunting smile. A grey "PENN STATE" shirt hangs over his frame, covering up his khaki shorts.

"May I ask who you are?"

"I'm a man with a box of books. But my friends call me Rich."

I dig through the titles, unfamiliar with most and disinterested with all.

Fire reaches from behind me to grab a small book at the top of the pile. I watch him turn it over in his hands, absorbing its every molecule. I see the title of the book, which unlocks a cascade of inner laughter.

The Short Path to Enlightenment.

Of course he would.

"Hey, that's a good one, my favorite," Rich calls out.

Fire drags his eyes upward, coming eye to eye with Rich's.

"Thank you."

He nods and walks off with the book under his arm.

My eyes roll, just for fun, before I return to the heirlooms.

---

90 The ashram community

***

"It says here that enlightenment can be obtained through surrendering the body," his monotone voice drills me deeper into the library couch.

"But what does that even mean?"

"Well, one must surrender all that is the body before enlightenment can be obtained."

I roll my head in a melodramatic fashion from one side of the couch to the other, landing my vision onto him.

"The only thing we are given in this damn life is a body, and you want me to surrender it?"

"Well, that's what the author is saying." He holds up his newly discovered bible.

"That's bullshit."

"And we must surrender emotions, too, such as anger and bitterness."

I bite my tongue and look the other way.

This is the shit that irritates me.

Since when did spirituality become about suppressing human emotions? This is the new-age conundrum people are falling victim to across the world. It irks me. Suppressing emotions like anger, grief, and sadness is equivalent to shoving a bomb up your ass and waiting for it to blow. It's not just unhealthy, it's dangerous. There's an inhumane flare to it, a robotic notion. Last time I checked, I have flesh, raw human flesh with raw human emotions, and I allow myself to experience them.

"I don't agree with that statement. I think we need to be more human and make more mistakes. Forget about surrendering the body. How about coming more into the body?"

He stares at me as if I've jabbed him.

"Well, what if we hurt someone throughout those mistakes?"

"Then we'll learn from it hopefully. If not, that's what hell is for, and hell isn't a place. It's a state of mind. Another word for it could be guilt or shame, which are emotions—human ones."

He keeps his brown eyes fixated and removes his obsessive "following" from *The Short Path to Enlightenment* right on over to me, landing his newfound path in my lap as if I'm the one who discovered alchemy. His eyes glaze over while absorbing my reflections, my awareness, and my experiences, readying to surrender himself as a student to my clumsy outbursts. I watch it happen, the moment when a parasite redirects its path, embedding itself into the truths of a new host.

"That's it. I want to be more human."

I see the opening and I take it.

"Well, then follow me."

My body comes alive and walks out the library door.

He chases behind, leaving *The Short Path to Enlightenment* on the couch.

***

We walk under the fresh moonlight, the street-lamps above us nearly blocking it out.

I don't look at him, but with my hands behind my back I walk and speak.

"When you, sir, close your eyes and meditate, you look to transcend your body. When I meditate, I look to acknowledge my body, to understand it. Without this vehicle, we wouldn't be able to meditate in the first place. I don't shoot for blackness and silence, but for colors and communication—from my spirit, of course—and through that I find a sense of calm because I get to know myself."

I take his hand in mine.

"What did you feel right there?"

"Calmness."

I pull him toward me so our faces meet.

"What do you feel right now?"

He smiles.

"Calmness."

I move in soft, not wanting to burn or be burned, letting my lips do something other than speak. Stillness glides past us, stoking the flames of passion which didn't exist just moments prior.

I pull away.

"How did that make you feel?"

No answer, just a shy smirk and blushing cheeks.

"Now, why would we want to suppress that?"

BURN WITH ME

—

Out in the middle of nowhere Pennsylvania is a wonderful place to spend the autumn season. Daylight simmers down to a periwinkle hue, hiding shyly each evening behind the forthcoming darkness. Clouds huddle close together, bringing dampness to the earth, blessing the last harvests of the season. The foliage undergoes transformation, teaching us the cycle of life and death is a beautiful thing.

More students show up to the ashram, which expands our task list exponentially. I've now become the head honcho in the kitchen, where I spend my days crafting plant-based meals for our guests, using up the last and most fruitful of our harvest.

I'm the mind behind the coconut creamed zucchini soup, garnished with dill and Himalayan sea salt. I'm the beating heart of the roasted squash, mushroom, and rosemary stew, a dish showcasing the flavors of autumn itself.

I roast our red peppers with cherry tomatoes. Under the heat they sizzle, their scent filling the halls and provoking ecstasy. I don't follow a recipe, but my own intuition, coupled with touch, taste, smell, sound, and sight. I'm learning as I go along. For instance, I discovered what happens when someone forgets to label certain (very spicy) ingredients (habaneros) in a community shared kitchen. But hey, we're all still alive and thriving.

With me in the kitchen, Fire's twenty-three-hour fasting experiment has been obliterated. He looks to me for dietary advice, in which case I've handed him a book called *Liver Rescue* by Anthony William and tell him to catch up. Morning times are for juicing celery, and fruits are crafted from the hands of God for human consumption. I cook; he eats—a lot. It's as simple as that. My mother would be an extremely proud woman if she were to see just how much of my food Fire inhales.

As a stubborn Italian woman typically refusing to let her family consume food outside of her own preparation, my mother always told me growing up, "Dee, the way to a man's heart is through his stomach." I recall one afternoon when she said these exact words and pointed her long wooden spoon right past my shoulder and directly at the table. There my two brothers were sitting across from each other, shirtless and in complete silence. They were devouring their second meatball sandwich, completely tamed by their own mother's spell.

***

I wipe down the kitchen counter and place the leftovers inside the fridge. From down the halls we can hear the retreating guests chanting in their lowest voices with their highest hopes. The lights of the kitchen flicker off, and I grab my cup of tea and head out the back door.

Up the hill I walk, careful not to spill a single drop. Letting the early chill satiate my bones, I take a seat on the bench where it all began, no longer allowing a gap. Fire drapes his woolen shawl over us, containing the warmth. Under the bright moonlight, the chorus of critters perform just for us. When we're silent, they're soft-spoken. When we speak, they provide the symphony.

"Deanna."

He waits for my full attention.

I give it to him.

"Yes."

"You were in my dream the other evening, and it was oddly real. We stood in the hall of the ashram and for whatever reason, it seemed as though you were angry with me." He pauses. "In the dream you actually were my partner. You were my girlfriend."

I remain silent.

"The reason you were angry at me was because I had been ignoring you." He stops his short description and brings his hand to my face, showing a vulnerability that's been hiding behind the shadow.

"I want you to know I would never ignore you. If I had the opportunity to have you as my partner, I would make sure you're always heard, always seen, always acknowledged."

Like a fool I swallow his words.

Something happens in the deep inner mechanics of a woman's mind when a masculine counterpart says these words to her, when they use things like "always" and "never" in the best of contexts. Something activates from her breasts to her brain and makes her drop down into her body and prepare for a life well-lived alongside this partner. The level of commitment a woman can access when she is committed to is the definition of loyalty.

It's what every woman wants, even if they refuse to admit it.

Loyalty and communication.

To be seen. To be heard.

He's showing me a personalized contract of love and I'm gleefully willing to sign my name across the page. Waiting to receive the love of someone who will see me for who I am—what more could I long for? This is why we sign up for love, because it's the most powerful teacher in the universe. It shows us ultimately just how much we value ourselves and how we value others. How considerate are we going to be with ourselves and the person in front of us? Love asks us to throw our souls into the flames, being vulnerable in order to receive the vulnerability of our lover.

My heart is endowed.

I have located my flame, and together we shall burn.

***

Because of our living situation, Fire and I are circumspect to not to let anyone in on the extent of our romance, though it's obvious by now. We wait until late in the evening, grabbing each other's hands and feeling the electrical current run through our fingertips. The amount of contact our eyes endure is enough to read the inner blueprint of one another, resulting in losing ourselves each night, only to be found the following morning during our group meditations.

Being around his presence becomes like a transcendental state, allowing me to withstand more intensified heat through every layer. Where my resistance toward Fire once resided now stands full-fledged desire and fascination. We rarely speak of it. In fact, we rarely speak in general, but I assume he feels a similar desire, as the restraint to keep his hands off me lessens fervently.

In the halls he whips me around passionately only to embrace me with his enchanted eyes and forgiving lips. In the car, on drives long or short, he wedges his way beside me, enticing me to pull over. Each breath, each meditation, each moment spent together, I slip behind the curtain, becoming the shadow created by the brilliance of his light.

I perceive him as mature, pure, and committed, someone who is ready to create a life together with me. He is certainly different than the guys of my past and his experiences are as mellow as his mood and his mind is clean. I wasn't aware this is what I wanted in a partner until now. I've certainly convinced myself that I'm smitten, but you know what they say:

"Only fools rush in where angels fear to tread. "

It's funny how we sometimes bite into the apple that never caught our eye.

How we convince ourselves that our fantasies are real.

How we tell ourselves "this is what I want."

***

"Take a seat. Make yourself comfortable, Deanna."

I move into her office, bowing my head, subtly asking for permission. She lifts her shawl and crosses her legs. Peering at me through her thin spectacles, she smiles with a face that asks but already knows.

"How is your internship going so far?"

I bite my tongue to hide my smirk, but feeling her gaze penetrate me, I fall short in succeeding.

"It's been really good."

"Oh, yeah. What're you enjoying about it?"

"Preparing the meals are my favorite."

She nods with squinting eyes, pressing further into my space.

"Oh, we love the way you cook. What are you learning about it?"

"A lot. Flavor combination. Portioning. Recipes. And so much more."

She keeps her legs crossed, hand under her chin and eyes unflinching.

"Can you tell me what you've been learning about yourself?"

Being the founder of the ashram, she has permission to ask me such things in such investigative ways, and I have no choice but to answer them. Living at an ashram means your privacy is the surrounding community's priority. Anything hidden results in a slap on the wrist, a side glance from the periphery, and a call into the office. I know why I'm being called in here. I do. Intimacy is not to be explored in any scenario while confined to these walls. You and I both know what happened underneath that fresh moonlight, and, well, that was only one scenario.

"Yes, I've been learning that..."

My head nods with the words I speak, searching for what to say under such pressure.

"Life has a funny way of teaching us."

"Can you explain that?"

"Well, I came here to learn about myself, but I've been more focused on others."

"I can tell. You two have quite the connection. Do you want to talk about it?"

Here is where I pause. Sure, I'll talk about it. But what the hell do I say? There isn't anything to share. I just happened to walk through the doors of a yoga center and this bizarre person appears seemingly out of nowhere. At first I disliked being around him, but now I cannot stop thinking about him. He intrudes my brain with his silence and infiltrates my heart with his perplexing simplicity. My attraction toward him is an acknowledged spell I cannot break, and shucks, I *think* I like it.

"No."

"I understand. But I would like to speak to you of it. Sometimes, Deanna, when we commit to the spiritual path, we're tested in ways we cannot understand or know until afterward. Sometimes things are placed on our paths as illusions, *Mayas,* so we must learn to decipher the difference between what is true and what is fantasy. Soon you will be leaving, correct?"[91]

"Yeah, in two weeks."

"Have you ever stopped to think about what that will do to him? How it will affect his mind and spiritual practice? He's been here for over a year and plays a large role in our community, and we can't have him distracted when you leave. It would challenge all of us here."

I nod.

"Think about the consequences of getting burned before you play with fire. Think about others, and not just about yourself and your desires."

"I will."

"Is that all or is there anything else you would like to discuss?"

I shake my head no.

Dismissed.

***

---

91 Illusions created by the Gods

I run down the hall, opening the doors to the library.

He isn't there.

I make my way to the cafeteria.

He isn't there.

I peek my head outside, to our little bench.

He isn't there.

I slip into the spacious meditation room, the one where we spend early mornings.

He is there.

I take a seat directly in front of him, awaiting him to come out of trance and acknowledge me.

Fifteen minutes pass.

I place my hand on his knee, ever so slightly.

"Hey, I need to talk to you about something."

His eyes flutter open, redirecting them from the darkness onto me.

"I need to talk to you about something, too."

His voice comes out a rasp whisper.

"Okay, what is it?"

He takes his sweet time, unfurling his legs from the meditation posture, bringing blood back to them. Finishing his stretches, he returns to the seated posture again and meets my gaze.

"So, yeah..." He starts off his sentence the way he always does. "I've been meditating on this and I've come to a conclusion."

I sit silent in my wild curiosity.

"It's time to tell you."

His eyes flicker, changing from one character to another, communicating to me the seriousness of his words, the finality of them.

"I'm leaving the ashram."

"Wait, what?"

"I'm leaving the ashram."

"When?"

"Next week."

My head shakes in disbelief.

"Where are you going?"

"To Montana."

"Oh, I'm shocked." My heart whimpers in its chest.

"Things are always changing, and we must allow for them to do so. So, what would you like to speak about?"

My breath catches up to me as I'm left hanging without an explanation.

"Well, it's about us."

He nods, eyes darkened.

"I was hoping we could be together after I leave, but it seems you've already got plans."

"Oh. I need to communicate something else."

"Yeah?"

"I'm not attracted to you."

"I don't understand."

"I'm not attracted to you, Deanna."

"But you made me believe you were."

"I made myself believe I was, and so did you. But this isn't going to work out. I already know."

My jaw drops in a quiet hysteria.

If you're confused, just think how perplexed I am. I willingly fell for a man who I thought was falling for me, who I really didn't want to fall for in the first place, and now he is the one leaving me? Can you believe this? Strange things occur in lust, and this happens to be one of them. My signature was short-lived, but the intimacy had been real, or maybe it was all the delusion of a flame that casts shadows against the brick walls of a vacant building.

"Shouldn't we talk about this?"

My voice is desperate.

His voice is relaxed.

"We just did."

"But just a few days ago things were different. So, this is it?"

"I've said everything I needed to, but if you have something to share I'm willing to listen."

My hand comes to my head.

"I'm such a fool for believing this could work. Look at you. You're constantly withdrawing from yourself. But you know what, a fool I am, but it's the fool who has the adventure, not the robot."

My jaw remains cracked open, now matching his as if our words have both uppercut each other.

Why would I fight for a man who is full of flight?

Why would I chase unavailable love?

He's spelled it out in black and white, the same colors he adorns his energy with.

Black and white.

Monotone.

Withdrawn.

I've fallen for a programming.

A robot.

A ghost flame.

SOME ICE FOR THAT BURN

When fire comes, fire burns, harsh, rash, and without reason. It creates its own pathway by destruction alone, unrelenting and unable to be controlled. The flames lure you in with their warmth, their dancing flickers, and once you are close enough it asks you to toss all you own into its center—your heart, your soul, your vulnerability. Mesmerized by the wavering tips of its luminescent glare, such a thing is not considered unrealistic.

We're all dying for passion. It's in the chemical component of our hormones. Our bodies run more ferociously on the idea of a good lover more so than consuming a good cup of coffee. We crave it. We need soft and tender human touch. We're born to be intimate, created to make love. The ability to feel pleasure alongside pain is not one of God's sick jokes, but one of humans perpetual requirements.

That's why we fall for those who have the power to both heal us and hurt us. They burn us so we can discover a way to create our own medicine. Abandonment, insecurities, lack of trust, dependency, rejection, jealousy—these are the sparks which douse the flames of love, turning it into the flames of uncomfortable, but necessary, growth.

When fire grows out of control, it chases us until it catches us by the shoulders, closing in, and whispers in our ear with its sultry way of being, "Are you ready yet?"

Are you ready to face your fears?

Releasing the things holding you back from experiencing what love actually is.

Are you ready to process the past?

Overcoming the pains that happened in childhood and onward.

Are you ready to feel?

Allowing yourself to not just experience the joy and pleasure, but the magnitude of pain.

The longer we take to answer, the longer we're being incinerated with every lasting second, refusing to see what we need to work on in order to reach the highest love possible.

Whether we like it or not, this is the pinnacle of relationships, folks. The culmination of the shadow. Just when you least expect it, it appears and shows you all the emotions you've been suppressing but have yet to become aware of. We need others to catapult us into those hard-to-reach places of our minds; we need others to "trigger" us. Without the contrast of others, we would be happy as a damsel drinking dandelion tea, but ignorant of the fact that this world is not just made up of one.

We can't think ourselves into love.

We also can't choose who we're going to fall for.

That's in the hands of a much more powerful source, but what we can control is how we allow ourselves to be valued, seen, and treated. What we can control is how we value, see, and treat others. The utmost attention should be given to these aspects, as healthy human relationships are the happiness meter to life itself.

You will not find gold in your career without it.

You will not find gold in personal projects without it.

And you certainly will not find gold in your spiritual practices if they are devoid of the one precious thing which assists us in growth the most.

Spiritual practices, however you choose to look at them, are a doorway, one that leads us through our worrisome minds so we can become more aware and evolve within. It's a beautiful process, but it's not done in vain. It's done for the sake of adding value to humanity, presence to people, and healing to the world. We become better humans so we can help others do the same, and vice versa. It's the way evolution works.

Iron sharpens iron.

We need each other.

Mr. Fire did not break my little heart. What he did, instead, was show me all the wounds I have yet to heal, all the wounds I showcased to the world without a damn foolish clue. Was he planning this? I think not. Lucky for me it happened fast, and with good reason, because who wants to linger in the flames? Burning up inside, rejected, ashamed, and abandoned, I took to the only thing I've ever had: my body and my emotions.

I let them burn. All of them. The rage, the guilt, the grief. The agony, the despair, the sadness. My body writhed under such revelations, such intensities. But this is what happens when we purge. It fucking hurts. I let myself burn in my own way, through the throes of humiliation, placing my very essence into the pit to watch it incinerate.

Now I'm watching it do something else.
Something indescribable.
Something worth noting.
After the flames of rage and grief simmered down.
After I explored this level of my shadow.
After I walked through my darkest memories.
A small light begins to gleam, right in the center of that pit.
A gentle calmness takes over.
A knowing is born.
Rebirth.

***

The first lesson of Fire is the lesson of values. What do you value, and how quick are you going to throw those things away for someone who doesn't value you? How we value ourselves creates the foundation of how others value us and vice versa. This is different than expectations, for expectations are quiet assumptions in the way one demands to be treated, which often leads to disappointments. Values are acknowledged standards which communicate to someone how you would like to be treated by showing them how you treat yourself as well as others. When we raise our values we raise our awareness, and when we raise our awareness, we evolve alongside the people who cherish us, alongside the people who have our back, and alongside our life-long partner.

The second lesson of Fire is the lesson of truth. Where did you acquire the truths you believe? Look behind the flames and see the origins of these belief systems in your mind. How outdated are they? Everyone has a truth, just like everyone has a brain. Each person's brain works in different capacities and octaves, just like each person's truth. Fire teaches us that hopping into the brain of someone else is destructive and a waste of precious time. The same goes for truths. By simply living our personalized truths, we expose others to theirs which, more likely than not, is going to be altered from yours. This doesn't mean force-feeding, scaring, or manipulating. This means simply being an example, an essence, or a breath of fresh air.

The third lesson of Fire is the lesson of rebirth. There comes a time in our lives when we are under the heat of the mighty flame. Everything is burning up around us, and maybe we cling on in hopes that we can salvage the tethered pieces. Let go. Let that sucker burn. Don't resist. Step aside and watch all you've worked for come down. It's the blessing of the phoenix, who comes to grace only those who are ready. It's an invitation. Fire teaches us sometimes the burning is necessary, for the perceptions of the past are only holding us down. Don't be afraid, for when the time is right a golden light will appear. You'll be graced by the phoenix, watching yourself rise from the ashes of your own vulnerability. You'll be rebirthed into a new way of life—a new you.

ETHER

OF ETHER AND EXPANSION

———

I stand and stare in awe at the pile of ashes laid out before me, smoldering with memories of four distant, and apparently necessary, lovers bubbling and oozing with stories told, past experiences, heartbreak, and growth.

I turn around with a clenched jaw, fistfuls of anger.

"Spirit, what the fuck?"

Her laughter rumbles in the distance.

"Woah, woah, Jersey girl. Calm down now. You're the one who signed up for this."

"But was that last one necessary? *Really*?"

"Uh, yeah, he was."

My arms fold over my chest.

"Why? I feel like you're just playing with me like prey at this point."

"*Ha*! Really, beauty? I tossed a pebble at your feet and you were naive enough to think it was gold."

I smack my palm to my forehead and turn my face the other way.

My spirit continues to speak.

"But you needed to experience that. You needed the test to formulate the awareness. I know shame comes at a realization such as this, but just think how exciting it'll be now that you'll truly know when you have found actual gold."

I fan my hand, dismissing her words.

"Trust me, it's coming."

This is enough to break my guard.

"When?"

"When you complete the final lesson."

"Goddammit!"

Now I'm really agitated.

"You're a feisty one to teach. Just listen. The four elements aren't complete without something else, something both beyond and within the shadows."

"You're freaking me out here."

"Don't be. Truth must be told, and the truth is there is a fifth element."

"Oh, God, please no."

"Yes. The element Ether. Ether is space, potentiality, and limitlessness. Ether is the void which allows for all things to exist, all paths to be possibilities, and all outcomes to be potentials. The way someone reacts to something, the decisions one makes, and the projects one creates are all sourced first from Ether and put into play by the combination of the other four elements."

"I get it. I get it. So, what's my task at hand?"

"Well..."

A swirling wind starts to pick up.

"There is one thing you'll need to access Ether."

A light drizzle begins coming down.

"You must embody it to truly learn your lessons."

The ground below me begins to rumble.

"Forgiveness. You must forgive them."

A fire ripples and crackles behind me, whipping my attention toward it.

"Go on. Forgive."

Standing naked in the dimming sun, exposed to all the raw elements, I curse to myself.

She wants me to forgive.

Really?

Who is there to forgive?

The wind blows harsher.

The drizzle turns to pour.

The ground aggressively shakes.

The fire before me roars loudly.

My eyes fall directly upon the flames, where the ashes of my vulnerability still lay scorched. I notice there is a strange glow rising from it, one that wasn't there before. It's alluring, mesmerizing in fact. It would look like heaven, if heaven had an appearance. The fire roars and spreads, growing grander by the minute, spreading my ashes as far as they can stretch. It growls like a hungry beast. I stand in silence until the edge of the flames crawl right on up to the tips of my barren toes.

I see a golden flash in the center, where my eyes stare hypnotized. It calls out to me without words, without whispers. It asks me to trust it, so I do. I take one step forward, feeling strangely lighter, putting an end to the heavy winds around me as I decide it's time for me to forgive Air. Another step takes place, bringing an end to the pouring rain, letting any past intensities wash away as I forgive Water. The third step grounds me, and a weight is notably lifted off my shoulders. The ground simmers to a gentle rumble as my forgiveness lands delicately upon Earth.

I find myself nearly in the center of the flames, protected from their scorching delight by some force emitting from my body. An object up ahead begins to appear, like an ethereal image, showing me what it is I'm walking toward. I only need to take one final and lasting step—the fourth step, the hardest one yet. I bite my tongue and grit my teeth. I thrash under the embarrassment, the shame, and the mortification. The flames close in on me. I can feel the heat licking my skin. The choice is mine. Perish in resentment or thrive in forgiveness. I hold my breath and take a lurch forward.

The flames stop.

Everything stops.

There is stillness.

There is silence.

The object now stands before me, appearing in full clarity.

It wavers in the gentle breeze, granting me access to see its form.

It's the outline of many pages.

I recognize it for what it is: a book.

But I don't know its meaning, nor its purpose.

"Deanna."

"Yes?"

"Now forgive yourself."

I drop down to my knees in a state of exasperation, in a state of tears.

I never thought that was an option, forgiving myself.

"Spirit," my voice is strained, "how do I do it?"

"Share what you've learned, in honor and humility. Share it all."

I pick the book up, turning it over in my hands.

A closer look tells me it's a story.

A story with many words.

A story of trust, adventure, and love.

A story of passion, growth, and humor.

A story of humans, lessons, and elements.

A story with my name on it.

I stand up, holding it in my hands, and as I do a blue flame appears, encircling me, but this time it's graceful and holy.

"Spirit, what happened to my shadow? Was this book birthed through it?"

"No. That comes from your forgiveness. Look up, darling."

Up ahead, I see what could only be a miracle.

Where my big shadow once loomed tall now stands another graceful blue flame, encircling someone else.

"Together you have the choice to walk into the Ether—into a space of creation, passion and joy. Deanna, meet the twin to your flames."

"What am I supposed to do with him?"

"Go deeper or go home, darling.

"This isn't a joke, is it?

"One can never be so sure about the shadow, as one can never be so sure about the light."

I ignore her statement and look up.

Tears moisten my brown eyes.

I can tell his blue eyes are experiencing the same.

All the lessons, all the winding roads, through the beautiful growth and the turbulent pain.

This is what it was all for. Was is worth it?

I take a step closer.

He does the same.

I reach out my arm.

He does the same.

I grab his hand, and together we walk into the Ether.

THE FOOL LAUGHS LAST

If you have yet to realize, this is the essence of the Fool.

Jack of all trades, master of fun.

The Fool is a maniac.

The Fool treads where others wouldn't dare peek and laughs when others wouldn't dare ponder.

The Fool is honored when humiliated, and humiliated when honored.

The Fool walks through Air, Water, Earth, Fire, and Ether because there are lessons to learn, people to meet, and places to see.

But more than anything, the Fool is forgiving to others and to herself. The Fool understands this life for what it is: an adventure where one can have access to growth through experiences. The Fool takes no one seriously, but others take the Fool very seriously. The Fool eventually transforms naivety into innocence by gaining wisdom through mistakes and by trusting decisions based on curiosity alone.

Sometimes the Fool disappoints others in her path for making topsy-turvy decisions, but hopefully her gentle nature and playful mind will teach the other person a lesson that the Fool knows very well: forgiveness. The Fool acknowledges she cannot teach everyone something, but she can learn something from everyone. The Fool has no goals but is enthusiastic, with one vision in mind: expansion.

The Fool wishes to know, seek, discover, delight, and understand.

The Fool wishes to live a life worth living.

**

I need to confess something to you, loyal reader.

The way I ended the stories in this book is not true to the endings which actually took place. No, not at all. I portrayed the endings as an ideal timing to learn my lessons, but let me tell you that wasn't the case. I clung, cried, cursed, slithered, resisted, and crawled my way through the elements, making the lessons of each relationship last as long as sanely possible. I made sure these lessons were affirmed and etched in my heart before I moved on.

Let's begin with Air. Remember that little bout of infidelity I spoke about? Instead of leaving, I greeted it with forgiveness and a willingness to learn about the depths of love and acceptance. Air and I stayed living in the small treehouse for ten months before taking off to travel across America. We then arrived in Asia together, where an obvious appearance of separate desires revealed themselves, sending me off to Laos and him back to Hawaii.

Next comes Water. I did leave Water on the balcony that day, watching him and his French military backpack walk off. This left me with his precious blanket and a head full of contemplation about who he was in my life and what he was teaching me. We reunited a week later which led, once again, to a separation during a flight to northern India. We went completely different ways. He stayed in India and Nepal, spending over nine months traveling and hiking with shepherds in the Himalayas all while thinking of me. I returned to America to process my trip all while thinking of him. We reunited a year later, only to smash up against the same wall, resulting in the same separation.

Here we have Earth, whose story is pretty on point, except for the observation of a few things. I stayed with him in Chiapas for a month after the cocaine and paranoia scene. We lived with a local named Ismael who hosted us generously until I was able to replace my debit card. Earth went back to Guatemala while I went to Mexico City. That was supposed to be the end, a graceful goodbye, but my heart couldn't handle it. Despite Ernesto's advice, I longed to laugh with him once more. I took a bus back down to Chiapas, awaiting his arrival which never came. He'd been detained while crossing the border and sent to a prison where he wrote "AMODEO" on the walls of the penitentiary. I helped to release him through ambitious phone calls, visits, and assistance through the energetic and spiritual realm.

We saw each other one last time in Antigua, the place where it all began, but this time I spoke full conversational Spanish. When my time to leave came, we both understood. He tattooed my lips on his back and we shed a few tears. On the day I left, I hopped on a bus and waved to him through the grimy window, then I watched him light up a smoke and walk away.

I did not separate from Fire when he threw his surprise plans at me in the ashram. Instead, he invited me a day later, asking me to join him and telling me that he was ready for a relationship. I abided with glee. Once we arrived in Montana, he weirdly began to withdraw, which made me push forward in confusion. The cycle repeated until he ended things with me two weeks into our relationship. Like a fool, I invited him to travel with me to Hawaii where he eventually told me the breakup was unnecessary. We tried again. About two months into that, during the writing of this book, he went cold once more, decided himself single, and left Hawaii without an explanation, goodbye, or a thank you.

That leads me to the writing of this book.

All along, during these adventures, I've been dying to write a book and frequently beat myself up for not making those efforts. Little did I know I was in the process of accumulating these stories to eventually write the words that you read on these pages. I was too naive at the time to understand that we must have contrast if we desire to create, experience if we desire to teach, and humility if we desire to share. When my life calmed down for a minute, the idea of writing this story through the four elements hit me like a freight train, and there was no turning back.

Shortly after, I landed in Hawaii where I planned to spend only a few weeks on a visit. A few weeks turned into a few months, which turned into over half a year, a long time for a Vagabond. It was here where I wrote my entire book, realizing that the story started and ended in quite literally the same place, on the Big Island of Hawaii, in South Kona, off a road called Nāpōʻopoʻo. I don't think this is a coincidence, as nothing in life ever is. I went through a turbulent time while writing this book, including but not limited to a breakup, unemployment, the pandemic, illness of a relative, death of a beloved dog, and intense shadow work. All of these things motivated the way I told the story, influencing and inspiring me up until the very end of this book's publication.

The concept of "standing up to the sun" came to me while writing the book. It's a metaphor for being on your "path," whatever that may look like. When we stand up to our own light, listen to our inner knowing and live a life full of curiosity, we open ourselves up to being both taught and delighted by anything and everything. Often the shadow steps forward, taking you through the deepest places in your mind to teach you lessons by bringing things into your life which reflect dark patterns. When this happens, do not ignore it. You're being asked to learn so that you can overcome the programmings, energies, and beliefs that hold you back from expanding who you truly are and from having your divine counterpart.

You may find a version of the "four elements" in your own life, be it relationships, jobs, traumas, and so on. May you honor them with humility and learn from your past, but most of all forgive, even yourself, so that you can bring awareness to your shadow and eventually access the unlimited potential of Ether.

Off the edge of the cliff, may we leap like great Fools into the Ether.

ACKNOWLEDGMENTS

I want to thank the entire world, but I'll first start off with thanking my parents, who have gifted me with the entire world and a life well worth living. Thank you Moo and Charles. I hope I still drive you crazy as your precious and wild middle child.

A special thank you to Tara Allen, the woman who picked up every single phone call throughout the writing of this book and who assured me that my writing does not suck but will one day teach and lead others. Tara, you are my illuminance, seeing in me the things I am blind to see in myself. I love you with a million suns.

Thank you to Lisa Kingry, the woman with the curly hair. Without you and your husband's generosity, this book would've never been created. You gave me a place of solitude to cultivate my thoughts and evolve my words.

An endearing thank you to the following whose conversations, life experiences, and light inspired me during the writing of this book: Jessica Blinman, Janet Nathani, and Steven Boutwell.

A special thank you to all those who interacted, supported, and cheered me on during my campaign for this book. Again, without your support, this book would've just been another crazy idea in my mind. I am beyond happy I've been able to bring something tangible out into the world. I hope this book inspires you to reach for the stars and grow:

Caitlin Flanagan, Kayla Strom, Michele Geyer, Sebastian Yepes, Chad Brown, Virginia Ellwanger, Cotah Rose, Sandra and Tim Heaton, Tiffany Mosher, Tierra Hopkins, Debbie Coke, Ashleigh and Brian Ecclestone, Jillian Leclercq, Laura Ruhle, James and Michelle Patton, Jack and Marilu Daum, Janet Nathani, Kristen Mendez, Natasha Burnham, Joyce Malanga, Amanda Daddario, Christine Nivet, Brenda Basilone, Swamini Shraddhananda, Katherine March, Linda Knapp, Jaclyn Snow, Tess Rumley, Nancy Bonta Voitko Evans, Hilary Flanagan, Eric Koester, Sandra-Janeth Cuellar, Jenny Bilskie-Smith, Richard Trosper, Joshua Voitko, Aaron Rovner-Buck, Carlos Moreno, Heather Carter, Dana Ching, Mark Jacobson, Johanna Treindl, Trey Humphreys, Angelica Flora, Michaela Ikeuchi, Jorge R. Alvelais, Dawn Keen, Lucas James McCain, Leslie and Howard Ling, Stephanie Grose, Mike Delangen, Hilda Staudinger, Chashi Oish Orjo, Annika Traser, Heather Gallop Cardoza, Laura Vanschaik, Aceneth Cole, Jasmine Mason, Cobie and Faye Hoek, Arianna Turso, Jennifer Connery, Tommy Milton, Danielle Hulsart, Kayla Finarelli, Serenity Chambers, Kyle Furlong, Aly Trione, Michelle Feathers, Allie Frank, Rebecca Rueter, Benjamin Cohn, Marlena Voudy, Cynthia Strauch, Amelia A Iacullo, Fernanda Mazariegos, Jon-Erik Jardine, Lara Printz, Shayna Craig, Carlo and Annette Amodeo, Josiah Pearl Kekai Camacho, Julia Stanley, Priyanka Surio, German Cisneros, Linsay Preston, Danielle Karwowski, Salvatore Orlando, Roos Lebbink, Joanna Scaparotti, Heather Reynolds, Krista Bruder, Yesenia Rodriguez, Ryann Hunt Bila,

Emily To, Brittany Spaulding, Natalie Bamford, Sarah Madden, Rachel and Charles Feenstra, Francesca Piethe, Staci and Linda Laubauskas, Dawn Frank, Claudia Duchene, Lynda and Rod Walker, Nicole Hulsart, Dorothea Dähn, Liana and Damiano Amodeo, Cassandra Bertolami, Tina Reilly, Joseph Amodeo, Reagan Breen, Laura Walker, Keely Yang, Melanie Gibson, Laurie Peer, Cassidy Federowski, Jon Harris, Kyrie Stern, Morgan King, Sonya Pearce, Michael Gerstein, Hunter Due, Athena Phan, Michael Winder, Chauntelle Sharp, Jessica Blinman, Camille Dentino, Patty Lassaline, Jason Guenther, Brian Segura, Rachel McGuinness, Siobhan Radway, Chris Barnett, Lulie Cottle, Marcela Zapari, Melissa Tirone, Angela Star, Samuel Moll, Lisa Francaviglia, Claire Musial, Randy and Josey Brendle, Paige Morton, Michael Amodeo, James Daum and Gustavo Gonzales.

Also, thank you to the four men who inspired this book. May you all find gold, wherever you tread.